TRAVEL

New York

p

TRAVELBUG

New York

Edited, designed and produced in 2006 by Automobile
Association Developments Limited for Parragon, Queen Street
House, 4 Queen Street, Bath BA1 1HE, UK

Published by AA Publishing (a trading name of Automobile
Association Developments Limited, whose registered office
is Fanum House, Basing View, Basingstoke, Hampshire,
RG21 4EA. Registered number 1878835).

ISBN-10: 0-7495-4648-4
ISBN-13: 978-0-7495-4648-9

Material in this book may have appeared in other AA
publications.

A CIP catalogue record for this book is available from the
British Library.

Printed and bound by Everbest, China

Find out more about AA Publishing and the wide range of
services the AA provides by visiting our website at
www.theAA.com

A02441

Contents

This book is divided into seven sections to cover the most important aspects of your visit to New York.

Essence of New York pages 10–11

10 Top Tips pages 12–13

10 Top Places pages 14–37
Our choice of the Top Ten attractions in New York, with practical information.

Discover pages 38–197

Two sections: New York and Excursions, each with brief introductions and a
listing of the main attractions

Practical information

6 suggested walks

Listings of the best places to eat and stay

Shopping and Leisure... pages 198–231

Listings of the best places to shop, take the children and be entertained.

What You Need to Know pages 232–249

A practical section containing essential travel information.

Maps

A list of the maps that have been used in this travel guide can be found in
the index on pages 250–253.

Prices

Where appropriate, an indication of the cost of an establishment is given by
$ signs:

$$$** denotes higher prices, **$$** denotes average prices, while **$ denotes
lower charges.

Many visitors arrive in New York already knowing exactly what they want to do and see. Climbing skyscrapers, going to Broadway shows, shopping, touring world-class museums and staying in luxury hotels can all be accomplished in New York with style and glamour. Yet this is a city of infinite guises, where contrasting neighborhoods house people from seemingly every nation and where local markets, secret parks, tiny museums and unsung architectural marvels await discovery at every turn.

If you only have a short time to visit New York, and would like to get a quick picture of the city, here are the essentials:

• **Visit the site of the World Trade Center**. A major new construction arising on the spot will be a memorial to those who perished on September 11 2001. The day will linger in the memory of New Yorkers for generations to come (► 57–58).

• **Go to the 86th-floor observation level**, by elevator or up the 1,575 steps, of the Empire State Building. The city's tallest building offers fabulous art deco features to rival the stupendous views (► 22–23).

• **Walk, bicycle, rollerblade or jog** through at least some of Central Park, one of the world's largest urban parks and without which New York really would be a concrete jungle (► 18–19).

• **Walk across the Brooklyn Bridge** (► 45), a major engineering feat of the 19th century and providing wonderful views of the Financial District skyline from across the East River.

• **Take the ferry** from Battery Park to Liberty Island. Security measures mean you can't climb the statue, but the grounds and pedestal are open to the public (▶ 36–37).

• **Go to a Broadway show** but do not pay full price; make use of the cut-rate ticket booths at Times Square (▶ 34–35).

• **Ride the Staten Island ferry** for the outstanding views of Lower Manhattan.

• **Hang the expense** and have a drink or dinner at Rockefeller Center's Rainbow Room (▶ 125, 132).

• **Stroll around Greenwich Village** on a Sunday afternoon and take a snack in the heart of the area, Washington Square Park (▶ 24–25).

• **Gaze at** Monet's *Water Lilies* or Van Gogh's *Starry Night* at the Museum of Modern Art (▶ 30–31), even if you look at nothing else.

Chrysler Building

Even in a city packed with architecture of great merit, the Chrysler Building stands in a class of its own. The definitive symbol of New York art deco and briefly the world's tallest building, the 1,045-foot-high Chrysler Building was completed in 1930 and remains one of the most distinctive features on the Manhattan skyline.

Reflecting the car manufacturing business of the building's owners and the era's enthusiasm for machine-inspired design, many features echo automobile design. Architect William Van Alen made the first large-scale use of stainless steel on a building exterior, employed hub caps as decoration on each setback and made the attention-grabbing spire resemble a car's radiator grille, complete with outward-leaping gargoyles.

Once partly used as a showroom for new

Chrysler cars, the lobby underwent a comprehensive restoration in the late 1970s. The work brought many features back to their original glory, notably the red-veined African marble walls and the elevators' plush laminated wood interiors. Although an observation level once existed at the base of the spire, there are now no public areas on the upper floors and visitors must content themselves with admiring Edward Trumbel's lobby mural depicting diverse images on themes of transportation.

The completion of the Empire State Building in 1931 robbed the Chrysler of its 'world tallest' status, though the title was only acquired in the first place through some slightly devious behaviour by Van Alen. The needle-like spire that tops the Chrysler Building's 77 storys was secretly assembled inside the tower and pushed through the roof. In doing so, Van Alen outwitted his former partner, H. Craig Severance, whose Bank of Manhattan Building (40 Wall Street), completed at just about the same time, would otherwise have earned the accolade.

✉ 405 Lexington Avenue 🕓 Mon–Fri 7am–6pm; closed holidays
🚇 Grand Central 🚌 42, 98, 101, 102, 104 ♿ Good ♨ Free

Central Park

Central Park, a mighty rectangle of green, is the soothing bucolic center of Manhattan's concrete jungle.

Filling 843 acres in the middle of Manhattan, Central Park evolved during the late 19th century as the visionary plans of Frederick Olmsted and Calvert Vaux took shape.

Creating glades, copses and rock outcrops, the landscaping also involved planting some 5 million trees and digging sunken roads. Fifth Avenue became a fashionable address as the wealthy erected handsome park-view mansions along the eastern side. For New York's poor, the park provided much-needed escape from sweatshops and filthy tenements.

The park continues to mirror the full range of New York life. Whether jogging, rollerblading, strolling or walking the dog, Manhattanites of all kinds relish its green spaces. Pick up a park map from the Dairy, built in 1870 and first used as a place where milkmaids dispensed milk to mothers and babies.

Cross the Sheep Meadow (which once really did hold sheep) for the Mall. Intended as a formal promenade, the Mall continues towards Bethesda Terrace and The Lake. Strawberry Fields is a tribute to musician John Lennon.

✉ Between 59th and 110th streets, and Fifth Avenue and Central Park West ☎ 212/310 6600 ◷ Always open; for safety, visit only during daylight 🍴 Tavern on the Green ($$$); snack stands 🚇 59th Street, 72nd Street, 81st Street, 96th Street, 103rd Street, 110th Street 🚌 1, 2, 3, 4, 5, 10, 30, 66, 72, 86, 104, Q32 ✋ Free

Grand Central Terminal

In 1939, as many people passed through Grand Central Terminal as lived in the entire U.S. The halcyon years of American rail travel saw Grand Central Terminal labelled 'the gateway to the nation'. As if to cement the terminal's metaphorical place at the heart of the nation's life, its name was (inaccurately) used as the title of a radio soap opera, Grand Central Station, first broadcast in 1937. Long-distance services no longer use the terminal; it is mostly commuters standing in line at the ticket booths inside the magnificent Main Concourse.

From an architectural viewpoint, there are few bigger, bolder or more beautiful places to buy a train ticket than Grand Central Terminal.

Said to be the largest room in the world, the Main Concourse measures 375 feet by 120 feet and enjoys a *beaux-arts* form allegedly modeled on the Paris Opera. Above, a 125-foot-high vaulted ceiling is decorated by artist Paul Helleu's interpretation of the zodiac constellations. Although architects Warren and Wetmore take credit for the Main Concourse, much of the terminal's design, including the innovative split-level concept, is thought to be the work of another architectural firm, Reed and Stem.

Facing Park Avenue, the terminal's main entrance is a slightly overbearing triumphal arch topped by sculptured Roman deities draped around an American eagle and arranged over a 13-foot-diameter clock.

✉ 42nd Street & Lexington Avenue ⏱ Always open 🍴 Restaurants ($$–$$$), cafés and snack stands ($–$$) 🚇 Grand Central 🚈 1, 2, 3, 4, 5, 42, 98, 101, 102, 104, Q32 ✋ Free ❓ Guided tours Wed 12:30 from Information desk on Main Concourse ☎ 212/935 3960

Empire State Building

Perhaps not the best or even the best loved, but the Empire State Building is certainly the world's best-known New York skyscraper.

Conceived in the booming 1920s but completed in the gloom of the Depression, the Empire State Building rose at a rate of four-and-a-half stories a week and was completed in just 410 days. By then, however, the Wall Street Crash had left few companies able to afford its rents, despite the prestige of being housed in the world's tallest building, at a height of 1,250 feet (a TV antenna added a further 222 feet in 1951). Through its early years, the building's only source of income came from visitors paying to sample the 80-mile panorama attainable on a clear day from its 86th-floor observation level.

While the views remain the chief attraction, the building is a major contributor to New York's catalog of art deco construction. From a base filling 2 acres, the five-story limestone-and-steel structure rises as a smooth-sided

EMPIRE STATE

shaft with windows set flush with the wall. Inside, the three-story lobby boasts marble walls and aluminium decoration, including the panels added in the 1960s depicting the 'eight' wonders of the world – the well-known seven plus the Empire State Building itself.

The 73 elevators include those designed to whisk sightseers to the observation levels at an astonishing rate of 1,400 feet per minute – it takes just seconds from the lobby to the 80th floor. The route by foot up 1,575 steps is undertaken annually in the Empire Step-Up race, completed by the fastest in just 11.5 minutes. Ordinary mortals take about half an hour just to walk down.

✉ 350 Fifth Avenue ☎ 212/736 3100 🕒 Daily 9:30–midnight 🍴 Snack bar ($) Ⓜ 34th Street 🚌 1, 2, 3, 4, 5, 6, 7, 16, 34, Q32 ♿ Good ✋ Moderate

Greenwich Village

The cafés, restaurants and bars of culturally vibrant Greenwich Village are a major element in Manhattan social life.

Created as a wealthy residential neighborhood in the 1780s, Greenwich Village then marked the northern extent of Manhattan's settlement and kept the rich away from the diseases sweeping through the poorer social stratas to the south. As the rich moved on, their vacated brownstone townhouses became apartments for newly arrived migrants who swiftly established businesses. By the turn of the 20th century, Greenwich Village was an ethnically diverse and socially tolerant area, with the low rents that helped attract the creative and unconventional members of what was later lauded as the first American Bohemia.

John Dos Passos, Eugene O'Neill and Edward Hopper were among the novelists, dramatists and artists that created Greenwich Village's cultural reputation. By the 1950s, Beat writers and abstract expressionist painters were gathering in the area's cafés. A decade on, Greenwich Village folk clubs saw the start of the protest movement – launching pads for musicians such as Bob Dylan.

Gentrification raised rents through the 1970s and 1980s and Greenwich Village people today are more likely to be lawyers or publishers than striving creative types. Nonetheless, the haphazard streets are a delight to stroll, packed with unusual shops and lined by well-tended brownstones.

At the heart of the action is Washington Square Park, a *mélange* of skateboarders, buskers and onlookers, above which stands the triumphal Memorial Arch.

✉ Bordered by 14th Street, Hudson Street, Broadway and Houston Street 🚇 W 14th Street or Christopher Street 🚌 1, 2, 3, 5, 8, 10

Metropolitan Museum of Art

Founded in 1870, this mighty museum is a vast collection of anything and everything of artistic value ever produced anywhere in the world. More than deserving of its reputation as one of the world's greatest museums, the Met's contents exhaust visitors long before visitors exhaust them. Use the ground-level information center and be selective. You can visit galleries that chart virtually the entire course of Western art. Memorable contributions include Botticelli's ground-breaking use of perspective with the *Annunciation*, and wonderful landscapes from Turner and Constable. Rembrandts and five of Vermeer's 40 extant paintings dominate the Dutch galleries, while El Greco's powerful *View of Toledo* stands out in the Spanish selections. The Impressionist and Post-Impressionist galleries hold noted works by Cézanne, Gauguin, Renoir and Van Gogh.

The influential paintings of the Hudson River School and a series of period-furnished rooms highlight the increasing self-assurance of American art as the country evolved into an independent nation. Among the strong points are a dazzling stock of Tiffany glasswork and a special section devoted to architect Frank Lloyd Wright.

With 40,000 objects dating from pre-dynastic times to the arrival of the Romans, the Met's Ancient Egyptian section begins with a walk-through reconstruction of the Tomb of Perneb and continues with case after case of immaculately preserved original exhibits.

Ten galleries are devoted to Islamic art, documenting the spread of Islam through intricate handiwork. Thousands of pieces highlight the skills of 9th- to 11th-century craftsmen in Egypt, Iran and Syria, and there is an enormous collection of ceramics unearthed by the Met's excavations at Nishapur, a 10th-century center of Islamic creativity.

Major assemblages of Roman and

Greek art, Chinese and Japanese ceramics, medieval European art (which continues at the Cloisters, ► 106), European arms and armor, the art of Africa, Oceania and the Americas, musical instruments, plus galleries of drawings, prints and photography, and modern art, consume only some of the rest of this vast museum.

Fifth Avenue ☎ 212/535 7710 🕔 Tue–Thu and Sun 9:30–5:15, Fri and Sat 9:30–8:45 🍽 Restaurant ($$) and café ($) 🚇 86th Street 🚌 1, 2, 3, 4, 18 ✋ Moderate (includes admission to Cloisters on same day)

Museum of Modern Art

Probably the world's best repository of modern painting and no slouch either with regard to sculpture, film and video.

When the Museum of Modern Art (MoMA) staged its first exhibition in 1929 the featured artists were not represented in the city and were considered too risky by the Met. Nonetheless 47,000 people attended the exhibition over four months. A decade later the Rockefeller family donated MoMA's present site.

Abstract expressionism accounts for some of the most noted holdings: Pollock's immense and spellbinding *One*, Rothko's shimmering blocks of color, works by De Kooning, and Motherwell's *Elegy to the Spanish Republic*. European contributions include Van Gogh's *Starry Night*, one of Monet's *Water Lilies*, Matisse's *The Dance*, Picasso's *Three Women at the Spring*, Braque's *Man With A Guitar and Woman with a Mandolin*, and Mondrian's *Broadway Boogie-Woogie* revealing the impact of New York's jazz rhythms and grid-style streets on the Dutch artist.

Some of these may be exhibited in the changing Collection Highlights gallery. From the late 1990s MoMA's approach to its holdings, so large that only around 12 percent could be exhibited, changed to a thematic focus.

✉ 11 W 53rd Street ☎ 212/708 9400; www.moma.org 🕐 Sat–Mon, Thu 10–5, Fri 10–7:45 🍴 Restaurant ($$$) 🚇 Fifth Avenue, 53rd Street 🚌 5, 6, 7, 18 ♿ Moderate (Thu& Fri 5.30–8.30 by donation)

Guggenheim Museum

The architecture might overpower the art but fans of both will find plenty to thrill them at this landmark museum.

Frank Lloyd Wright's stunning Guggenheim Museum has been a daring addition to the Fifth Avenue landscape since the late 1950s, its curves and horizontally accentuated form totally at odds with the traditional architecture all around. The innovations continue inside where, rather than being hung in room-like galleries, the exhibits are arranged along a spiral ramp, allowing visitors to start at the top and steadily make their way down.

Many New York millionaires lavished fortunes on art, but Solomon R. Guggenheim differed from the rest by switching from old masters to invest his silver- and copper-mining wealth into the emerging European abstract scene of the 1920s. Guided by Baroness Hilla Rebay von Ehrenweisen, a champion of the new movement in art, Guggenheim acquired works by the major exponents such as Léger, Gleizes and Delaunay, and a spectacular stash of paintings by Vasily Kandinsky. With these works and others hanging on the walls of his apartment at the smart Plaza Hotel, Guggenheim set up a foundation in 1937 to promote public appreciation of abstract art that eventually grew into the present-day museum, which opened in 1959, ten years after Guggenheim's death.

Selections from the Guggenheim collections, which also include Klee, Mondrian, Braque, Malevich and Modigliani, are shown on rotation and share space with high-quality temporary exhibitions. A broader selection of art is displayed in the Thannhauser Tower, a 1992 addition with a permanent exhibit of the acquisitions of art collector and dealer Justin K. Thannhauser. These include important pieces by Degas, Picasso, Van Gogh and Cézanne, and amusements such as Henri Rousseau's bizarre work, *The Football Players*.

✉ 1071 Fifth Avenue ☎ 212/423 3500 🕐 Sat–Wed 10–6, Fri 10–8. Closed 25 Dec, 1 Jan 🍴 Café ($–$$) Ⓜ 86th Street 🚌 1, 2, 3, 4, 18

Times Square

If a single spot yells 'this is New York' to the world at large, it is Times Square with its towering, animated neon signs.

A gathering place each New Year's Eve and the heart of the theater district, Times Square is a frenetic, gaudy and until the late 1990s rather seedy junction whose fame far outstriped its actual appeal. The area fell into social decline after World War II, but a major campaign to clean it up met with considerable success.

The square was revivied with a new development of hotels, shopping malls and office blocks, and the restoration of historic theaters. Retail franchises and theme restaurants dominate the area, which is patrolled by an unarmed security force.

Times Square acquired its name in 1904 when the *New York Times* offices were built there. By the 1920s, the theater district was established on adjacent streets. Raised in the heyday of vaudeville, many of the plush theaters remain.

✉ Between Broadway and Seventh Avenue, and 42nd and 47th streets 🚇 Times Square 🚌 5, 6, 7, 10, 42, 104 ❓ Free guided walking tours Fri at noon from Times Square Information Center, 1560 Broadway (between 46th and 47th streets) ☎ 212/768 1560

Statue of Liberty

The potent and enduring symbol of the U.S. as the land of opportunity – the Statue of Liberty.

Nowadays it is strange to think that an American emblem known worldwide was initially intended by its creator, Frenchman Frédéric-August Bartholdi, to stand in Egypt above the Suez Canal. The plans were rejected, but in 1871 on a visit to New York, the sculptor found the perfect site for his torch-carrying lady – at the entrance to the city's harbor. Equally surprising in retrospect is the antipathy towards the project on the American side following the decision for costs to be shared between France and the U.S. as a sign of friendship and shared democratic ideals.

As the lady, formally titled *Liberty Enlightening the World*, took shape in Bartholdi's Paris studio, the pedestal – the responsibility of the U.S. – made slow progress due to lack of funds, which prompted newspaper publisher Joseph Pulitzer to mount a campaign to raise money through small donations. The finished statue arrived in New York in June 1885 and Pulitzer announced that $100,000 had been collected. The lady was duly placed atop the pedestal and unveiled in May the following year.

Ferries to the 151-foot-high statue leave regularly from Battery Park. Once ashore, visitors not only have an excellent view of the lower Manhattan skyline but can tour the Statue of Liberty museum (and find a slightly higher view of the same skyline) on the 16-storey-high pedestal level. Exhibits document the history and symbolism of the statue, while the interior of the statue itself can be glimpsed through a glass ceiling. Further access is not possible.

✉ Liberty Island ☎ 212/269 5755 (ferry information); 212/363 3200 (statue information) 🕐 Daily 🍴 Cafeteria ($) 🚢 Battery Park ✋ Moderate ❓ Audio tours

Manhattan

Manhattan may only be a part of New York City, but as far as the world is concerned Manhattan is New York. For visitors from near and far, this long slender island is everything they ever imagined New York to be. Times Square, Broadway, Central Park, the Empire State Building, the Museum of Modern Art and everything else that defines New York to the world at large has a Manhattan address and entices travelers to spend day after day tramping its streets with a sense of wonder.

Once acclimatised to the wailing police sirens, the cruising yellow cabs, the street food vendors, legions of office workers crossing the road as one, and the general commotion that fills many a Manhattan street, newcomers will find themselves steadily discovering another Manhattan: one of neighborhoods with a village-like insularity harboring undiscovered attractions on quiet residential streets.

DOWNTOWN MANHATTAN

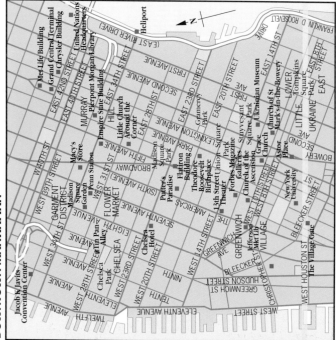

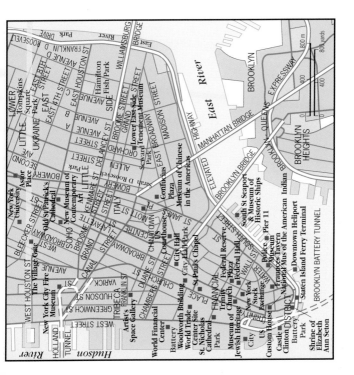

43

DISCOVER DOWNTOWN MANHATTAN

Downtown Manhattan is home to Greenwich Village with a rich cultural legacy and a major concentration of restaurants, bars, nightclubs and unusual shops. Farther south is SoHo, centre of the world art market during the 1970s, while much of Lower Manhattan is consumed by the Financial District.

BATTERY PARK

Providing 22 acres of greenery on the edge of the Financial District, Battery Park also holds a fair share of New York history, some of the details of which are supplied by the texts affixed to its lampposts. Created in the 18th century, the park's name stems from the cannons that once lined State Street, now framing the park but previously marking the Manhattan shoreline. The park's Castle Clinton, site of the ticket booth for Statue of Liberty ferries, was completed in 1811.

✉ Bordered by Battery Place and State Street ◑ Always open; visit during daylight 🍴 Snack stands ($) Ⓡ Bowling Green ✋ Free

BROOKLYN BRIDGE

Completed in May 1883, the Brooklyn Bridge provided the first fixed link between Brooklyn and Manhattan and, with a total length of 6,775 feet, it became the world's longest suspension bridge. The twin Gothic stone arches that rise 272 feet give the bridge great aesthetic appeal, though the most memorable aspect is the view of the Manhattan skyline as you cross from Brooklyn. Walkers, rollerbladers and joggers regularly cross the bridge; in 1884 21 elephants did the crossing in a stunt led by circus owner P. T. Barnum.

✉ Between Manhattan and Brooklyn ⏰ Always open Ⓜ Brooklyn Bridge ✋ Free

CHELSEA

The heart of Chelsea is around the junction of 23rd Street and Eighth Avenue, busy with shops, restaurants and art galleries since a 1990s regeneration made it one of Manhattan's most energetic neighborhoods. On Chelsea's western edge, many former warehouses were converted into viewing spaces for the work of new artists, making the area a major showplace for emerging art. In the same section, four early-1900s cruise-ship docks have been redeveloped as Chelsea Piers, offering sports activities, dining and shopping, beside the Hudson River.

✉ East of Fifth Avenue between 14th and 34th streets

CHELSEA HOTEL

The Chelsea Hotel has played an important role in New York cultural life, providing accommodation for artistic and literary notables since opening in 1905. Featured in Andy Warhol's movie *Chelsea Girls* in the 1960s, the hotel also earned a place in punk rock history as the venue of Sid Vicious's alleged murder of his girlfriend. The hotel's lobby is strewn with artworks from former guests.

✉ 222 W 23rd Street

☎ 212/243 3700 🕐 Lobby always open

🚇 23rd Street

✋ Free

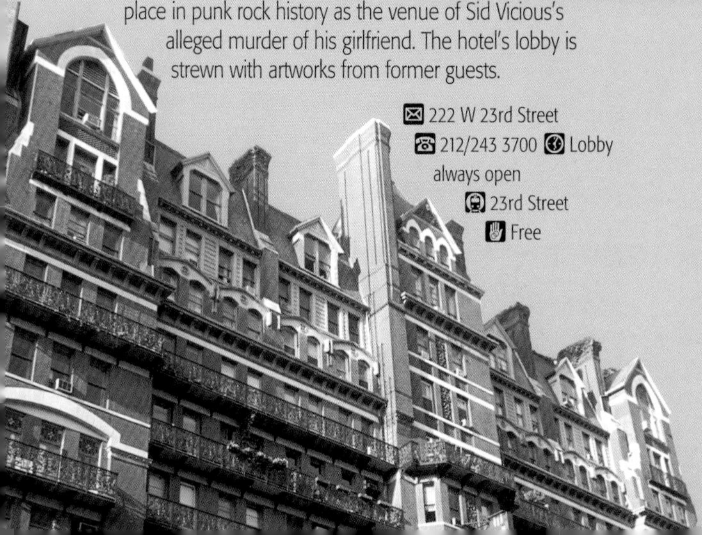

CHINATOWN

An estimated 150,000 people, mostly Chinese but also Vietnamese, Cambodians and Laotians, live in the tight-knit streets of Chinatown, lined by restaurants, herbalists shops and stalls laden with exotic foodstuffs. Chinatown became established during the 1890s but began expanding beyond its traditional boundaries when the easing of immigration restrictions in the 1960s brought a major influx of settlers from Hong Kong and Taiwan. Numerous banks and busy stores reflect the economic vibrancy of the area.

✉ Loosely bordered by Broadway, Bowery, Grand and Worth streets

🚇 Canal Street

walk

A WALK AROUND CHINATOWN

This flourishing ethnic neighborhood, greatly expanded by increased Asian immigration since the 1960s, is one of the largest Asian communities outside Asia and one of Manhattan's most densely populated quarters.

Walk south along Mulberry Street from Canal Street.

The crowds and market stalls along Canal Street are an indication that you are approaching the heart of Chinatown. Call into the Museum of Chinese in the Americas. South of the museum is Columbus Park, a rare instance of greenery in Chinatown.

Continue south along Mulberry Street and turn left along Park Street.

On the corner of Park and Mott streets is the Church of the Transfiguration (early 1800s).

Turn right along Mott Street to Chatham Square.

Directly across the square is the 17th-century First Shearith Israel Cemetery, Manhattan's oldest Jewish graveyard.

Turn left across Chatham Square and left into Doyers Street.

Lined by restaurants, Doyers Street terminates at Pell Street, first rounding the bend which provided an ambush point during the early 20th-century battles between the rival Chinese–American secret societies known as Tongs.

Turn right along Pell Street to the corner with Bowery.

At 18 Bowery, the Edward Mooney House was completed in 1789 and is the oldest surviving Federal-style house in Manhattan.

Turn left from Bowery into Canal Street.

Distance 1 mile **Time** 2–4 hours
Start/end point Canal Street **Lunch** Joe's Shanghai (➤ 83)

CITY HALL

When designed in 1803, City Hall was intended to mark the northern edge of Manhattan, but nine years later at the time of its completion, it was already engulfed by fast-expanding New York. Raised in a mixture of Federal and French Renaissance styles, the dainty building retains its civic role but its form seems entirely incongruous within the modern metropolis. Inside, council members go about their business and temporary exhibitions document various aspects of city history.

✉ Broadway at Murray Street ☎ 212/788 3000 🕐 Mon–Fri 9–4 🚇 City Hall ♿ Few 🖐 Free

EAST VILLAGE

Unorthodox lifestyles, unconventional beliefs and uncompromising modes of dress have long been part of the East Village. Leon Trotsky propagated Bolshevik revolutionary views from a basement printing press here in the 1910s, Beat Generation gurus arrived in the 1950s, hippies in the 1960s, and punks in the 1970s. Although much gentrification is evident, black leather, nose rings and tattoos are still far from unusual.

Within the East Village is the long-established ethnic pocket of Little Ukraine, and the more recent Little India along Sixth Street, a center for Indian cuisine.

✉ Loosely bordered by Fourth Avenue, Bowery, First Avenue, 14th and Houston streets 🚇 Astor Place

LITTLE UKRAINE

While the East Village (► 53) embraces one counter-cultural phenomena after another, one section of the neighborhood that has stayed relatively constant since the late 19th century is Little Ukraine. Enforced conscription into the army of the tsar resulted in many Ukrainians fleeing their Russian-dominated homeland and settling here, establishing what, by 1919, was the largest urban Ukrainian community in the world.

A handful of restaurants specializing in *borscht* and *blintzes*, and a few craft shops offering *pysansky* (hand-painted eggs) reflect the East European character, while St George's Ukrainian Catholic Church, 16–20 E 7th Street, provides a community focal point.

✉ Centered on Second Avenue between Fourth and 14th streets 🚇 Astor Place

FINANCIAL DISTRICT

New York's Financial District is the heartbeat of the U.S. economy and a leading player in the global marketplace, yet many of the high-rise towers of commerce that litter the neighborhood sit side-by-side with markers to a time when populated New York barely reached beyond today's Greenwich Village. Peek inside the 18th-century St Paul's Chapel (on Broadway facing Fulton Street) to see George Washington's favorite pew, and pay respects to Alexander Hamilton, the U.S.'s first treasurer, buried in the 17th-century graveyard of Trinity Church (on Broadway, facing Wall Street).

✉ South of Chambers and Fulton streets

Ⓢ Bowling Green, Broad Street, Cortland Street, Fulton Street, Nassau Street, Rector Street, South Ferry, Wall Street or Whitehall Street

walk

A WALK AROUND THE FINANCIAL DISTRICT

All of populated Manhattan was once contained within the boundaries of today's Financial District, where historic churches sit amid a forest of skyscrapers and markers to two disasters.

From South Street Seaport (▶ 75), walk to the junction of Fulton and Water streets.

An unprepossessing model lighthouse serves as a memorial to the 1912 sinking of the Titanic.

Walk west along Fulton Street for St Paul's Chapel, immediately across Broadway.

Completed in 1766, St Paul's Chapel is the only pre-Revolutionary church in Manhattan. Preserved inside is the pew used by George Washington following his inauguration as the U.S.'s first president in 1789. Following the destruction of the World Trade Center in September 2001, the chapel was

covered with handmade memorials to the dead. A block west across Church Street, new construction and a planned memorial occupy the site of the World Trade Center.

Walk south along Broadway to Trinity Church.

At the junction with Wall Street stands Trinity Church, completed in 1846 and the third church on the site. Inside is an excellent small museum; the graveyard holds the tomb of Alexander Hamilton, the U.S.'s first treasurer.

Walk east along Wall Street, turning right into Broad Street.

Wall Street's name derives from the barricade erected by Dutch settlers in 1653 to repel the British. At 20 Broad Street stands the New York Stock Exchange (► 70), the linchpin of the U.S. economy. Facing the exchange on Wall Street is Federal Hall National Memorial.

Distance 1 mile **Time** 2–4 hours **Start point** South Street Seaport
End point Federal Hall National Monument
Lunch Bennie's Thai Cafe (► 85)

GRAMERCY PARK

Enclosed by 19th-century brownstone townhouses, Gramercy Park is New York's only private park.

A stroll of the perimeter passes several notable buildings: the National Arts Club (15 Gramercy Park South) was occupied by state governor Samuel Tilden during his campaign against the notoriously corrupt Tweed ring in the 1870s; the Players Club (16 Gramercy Park South), marked by two ornamental theatrical masks, was an influential thespians' organization founded by actor Edwin Booth, remembered by a statue in the park which depicts him immersed in the role of Shakespeare's *Hamlet*.

✉ Between Irving Place and Lexington Avenue, bordered by E 21st and 22nd streets ⏰ Only open to local residents and guests of Gramercy Park Hotel 🚇 23rd Street ♿ None ✋ Free

walk

A WALK AROUND GREENWICH VILLAGE

While unmatched for restaurants and nightlife, Greenwich Village's artistic and literary past is also well in evidence on narrow streets lined with dainty houses.

Begin at Grace Church.

Designed by James Renwick, Grace Church was completed in 1846 in Gothic Revival style. The church marks Broadway's most southerly bend, a deviation in the otherwise straight route caused by a Dutch settler's refusal to let the road cross his land.

Walk west along 10th Street. Across the junction with Fifth Avenue is the 1840 Church of the Ascension. Continue south along Fifth Avenue.

At the foot of Fifth Avenue is Washington Square Park's Memorial Arch, bearing a likeness of George Washington.

Walk west along Washington Square North, then turn left into Macdougal Street and walk south.

Macdougal Street, south of Washington Square Park, holds numerous restaurants, including Caffè Reggio at number 119.

Continue along Macdougal Street, turning right into Bleecker Street.

Bleecker Street is lined by shops and restaurants and is particularly good for evening strolling.

Cross Seventh Avenue and turn left into Barrow Street.

Barrow Street and its neighbours, such as Bedford and Commerce streets, hold many attractively maintained 19th-century homes.

Return to Seventh Avenue and walk north, turning right along Christopher Street.

At the junction with Greenwich Avenue stands the Jefferson Market Courthouse, completed in 1877 in a mix of Gothic styles. The building is now a public library.

Distance 2 miles **Time** 1–4 hours **Start point** Grace Church
End point Christopher Street **Lunch** Mama Buddha (➤ 90)

LITTLE ITALY

Today, only a few thousand Italians remain in Little Italy, an area that between 1890 and 1924 absorbed some 145,000 immigrants from Sicily and southern Italy and became awash with Italian restaurants and cafés. Over subsequent decades, Italians from the area became ingrained in the social fabric of New York life. Italian–American New Yorkers that grew up in Little Italy still regard it as a spiritual home, although increased prosperity prompted a mass movement away from the neighborhood's tenement homes to more comfortable suburban living.

Undoubtedly the best time to visit Little Italy is during September's Feast of St Gennaro, when the compact area regains something of its effervescent past.

✉ Bounded by Canal–Houston streets and Eliizabeth–Lafayette streets 🚇 Spring Street

LOWER EAST SIDE

No part of Manhattan resonates with the immigrant experience
more than the Lower East Side. From the mid-19th century,
the high-rise tenements of the Lower East Side became
crowded with successive waves of new arrivals: Irish, Germans,
East Europeans, and Jewish settlers who made the Lower East
Side the largest Jewish settlement in the world by the 1920s.

Nowadays, Orchard Street is noted for its discount clothing
outlets and nearby Essex Street for its fruit and vegetable
market. Much of this never-fashionable area's early buildings
remain, though a number have been torn down and replaced
with largely unattractive, high-density housing blocks.

Reflecting changing patterns in immigration, many of the people who live here now are Spanish-speaking, mostly from Puerto Rico.

✉ East of Bowery, south of Houston Street Ⓜ Delancey Street

LOWER EAST SIDE TENEMENT MUSEUM

A cramped, rat-infested apartment shared with several other families was what awaited many arrivals to the Lower East Side in the 19th century – and for most it was far better than the conditions they had left behind in an oppressive Europe.

To get an inkling of early immigrant life in New York, visit this excellent museum which occupies an 1863 tenement building and is furnished to replicate the living conditions then. Exhibitions reveal diverse facets of local life and document the otherwise seldom acknowledged hardships faced by the Lower East Side's arrivals from Asia and Latin America.

✉ 90 Orchard Street ☎ 212/431 0233 🕔 Guided tours only: Tue–Fri every 40 mins from 1:20–4:45; Sat and Sun every half hour from 11:15–4:45 Ⓜ Delancey Street ♿ Few ✋ Moderate ❓ Guided walks Apr–Dec Sat and Sun

NATIONAL MUSEUM OF THE AMERICAN INDIAN

Although its holdings are slowly diminishing due to the insistence of many Native American groups for the return of their cultural treasures, the stock of this excellent museum, also called the George Gustave Heye Center, spans the diverse indigenous cultures of North, South and Central America. Among the baskets, quilts, pottery and other items of artistic, spiritual and cultural importance are some of the documents that paved the way for European colonisation of Native American lands. In a curious juxtaposition, the museum occupies an elegant *beaux-arts* building that formerly served as the U.S. Custom House.

✉ 1 Bowling Green ☎ 212/514 3700 🕐 Daily 10–5, Thu 10–8
🚇 Bowling Green ♿ Good 🎟 Free

NEW YORK CITY FIRE MUSEUM

Fires were the scourge of early New York and so too, in many cases, were the firefighters. Before the creation of a municipal fire service in 1865, fire crews were privately hired and usually comprised members of rival gangs whose members fought each other before fighting the fire in anticipation of a reward.

The intriguing story of the city's fires and those who tried to put them out is told here over three floors with an entertaining collection of horse-drawn carriages, hose-pipe nozzles, axes, ladders, dramatic photos and New York's first fire bell.

✉ 278 Spring Street
☎ 212/691 1303
🕐 Tue–Sat 10–5, Sun 10–4 🚇 Broadway–Lafayette or Bleecker Street ♿ Few
✋ Donation

NEW YORK STOCK EXCHANGE

Within the neo-classical façade that overpowers Broad Street is the high-tech money market of the New York Stock Exchange. Wearing the brightly colored jackets that indicate their particular job, brokers, reporters and pagers stride purposefully around the 37,000 square feet of trading floor, their successes and failures affecting the value of currency around the world. The famous story of stockbrokers leaping from the high windows of the building during the 1929 Wall Street crash in entirely untrue.

✉ Broad Street ☎ 212/656 5168
Ⓠ Broad Street or Wall Street ♿ Good
✋ Free

OLD ST PATRICK'S CATHEDRAL

Old St Patrick's Cathedral, completed in 1815, served the spiritual needs of the Irish population that inhabited the immediate area before the ethnic turnaround that transformed the neighborhood into Little Italy.

The Gothic-style cathedral was seriously damaged by fire in 1866 and lost its place as the city's Roman Catholic see with the consecration of its far grander namesake in Midtown Manhattan (▶ 134) in 1879. Though unspectacular, the intimate interior makes for a few welcome minutes of respite from the city frenzy.

✉ 263 Mulberry Street ☎ 212/226 8075 🕐 Call for times 🚇 Spring Street ♿ Few 💷 Free

PIERPONT MORGAN LIBRARY

J. Pierpont Morgan, a major figure in late 19th-century New York, lavished some of his fortune on manuscripts, rare books and drawings. Among the many treasures gathered here are Gutenberg Bibles, a Shakespeare first folio, a signed manuscript of Milton's *Paradise Lost* and handwritten works by Bach, Brahms and Schubert. The setting is magnificent. The library is undergoing renovation and is due to reopen in 2006.

✉ 29 E 36th Street ☎ 212/685 0610 🚇 33rd Street ✋ Moderate

POLICE MUSEUM

The fabled mean streets of New York have produced more than their share of notorious villains, and many of them are recorded here, as are the officers who brought them to justice. The machine gun belonging to New York-raised gangster Al Capone is one prized possession, but this museum also carries vintage handcuffs, truncheons, precinct logbooks and a terrifying assortment of weapons collected in amnesties.

✉ 100 Old Slip ☎ 212/480 3100 🕐 Tue–Sat 10–5 🚇 Fulton Street
 Donation

SOHO

In one of the transformations that regularly regenerate Manhattan neighborhoods, the previously derelict 19th-century factory buildings of SoHo became the center of the world art market during the 1970s. A few years earlier, the well-lit spacious buildings had been attracting artists. As several new New York artists became internationally recognized, millionaire collectors arrived to snap up their works as galleries opened on every street. The galleries remain, alongside chic clothing stores and restaurants, but most SoHo residents today are lawyers and media professionals.

✉ South of Houston Street, between Sixth Avenue and Broadway

🚇 Prince Street or Spring Street

SOUTH STREET SEAPORT

Through the 18th and 19th centuries, the center of Manhattan's maritime trade was around the area now taken by South Street Seaport. This mix of shops and restaurants beside the East River sits alongside historic ships and nautically themed museums. The area and its old ships – among them the 1911 *Peking*, a four-masted cargo vessel which can be boarded – is enjoyable.

✉ Museum, Fulton Street
☎ 212/748 8600 ⏰ Daily 10–5
🍴 Cafés/restaurants ($–$$)
🚇 Fulton Street or
Broadway–Nassau Street ♿ Good
✋ Moderate

THEODORE ROOSEVELT BIRTHPLACE

Theodore Roosevelt, the only U.S. president to have been a native of New York City, was born to a prominent family at this address in 1858. Although the building of that time was demolished, what stands now is a detailed reconstruction of the childhood home of the nation's 26th president and contains many of the family's furnishings. A detailed chronology of Roosevelt's life outlines his numerous achievements, not least his acquisition of national popularity after leading the so-called Rough Riders during the 1898 Spanish–American War.

✉ 28 E 20th Street ☎ 212/260 1616 🕐 Tue–Sat 9–5 🚇 23rd Street
✋ Moderate

TRIBECA

Echoing the gentrification that transformed neighbouring SoHo in the 1970s, TriBeCa was, during the early 1980s, steadily colonized by artists who created living and studio space in buildings that once housed the city's poultry and dairy industry. Very soon, rising rents priced out the artists, and developers created chic loft apartments for well-heeled tenants. Serving the new population, TriBeCa's streets acquired fashionable restaurants, expensive boutiques and other services regarded as essential by the affluent and style-conscious New Yorker.

✉ South of Canal Street, between Broadway and the Hudson River

🚇 Chambers Street or Franklin Street

UNION SQUARE

Restyled in the 1980s, Union Square holds a popular farmers' market three times a week where fruit, vegetables, cheese and bread are sold from stalls. It is ringed by fashionable eateries: a far cry from the 1970s when years of neglect had turned it into a seedy drug dealers' haunt.

Created in the early 1800s, Union Square was originally at the heart of fashionable New York life but, as high society moved northwards, it became a focal point for political protest. By 1927, police had taken to mounting machine-gun posts on surrounding rooftops and, in 1930, no less than around 35,000 people protested here against unemployment.

✉ Bordered by Park Avenue, Broadway and 14th Street 🚇 14th Street–Union Square
✋ Free

WOOLWORTH BUILDING

The world's tallest building for 16 years, the Woolworth Building – headquarters of the retail organization – was officially unveiled in 1913 by president Woodrow Wilson who flicked a switch and bathed the building in the glow of 80,000 electric bulbs.

Leering gargoyles decorate the 800-foot-high tower but the real highlight is the lobby. Go inside to relish the blue, green and gold mosaics on the vaulted ceiling and the sculptured caricatures of the building's architect, Cass Gilbert, and its original owner, F. W. Woolworth.

✉ 233 Broadway 🕐 Lobby Mon–Fri 7–6 🚇 City Hall or Park Place ♿ Good 🖐 Free

Where to eat & drink...
Downtown Manhattan

CHELSEA

BOTTINO ($$–$$$)

Among the trendiest eateries in Chelsea, offering mostly
Tuscan-influenced fare and especially strong on seafood.

✉ 246 Tenth Avenue ☎ 212/206 6766 🕙 Lunch and dinner
🚇 23rd Street

CHELSEA GRILL ($–$$)

Neighborhood favorite offering quality diner food in a
comfortable setting; the burgers have many admirers.

✉ 135 Eighth Avenue ☎ 212/242 5336 🕙 Lunch and dinner
🚇 14th Street–Eighth Avenue

EIGHTEENTH AND EIGHTH ($–$$)

American and Caribbean fare; low prices, large portions and
gregarious atmosphere, best sampled at the weekend brunch.

✉ 159 Eighth Avenue ☎ 212/242 5000 🕙 Breakfast, lunch and
dinner 🚇 18th Street

EMPIRE ($–$$)
Dependable round-the-clock diner.
✉ Tenth Avenue at 22nd Street ☎ 212/243 2736 🕐 Open 24 hours
🚇 23rd Street

CHINATOWN

BO KY ($)
Unpretentious noodle shop with tasty soups; good prices.
✉ 80 Bayward Street ☎ 212/406 2292 🕐 Breakfast, lunch and dinner 🚇 Canal Street

GOLDEN UNICORN ($$)
A favorite for large family banquets or big parties. Dishes from appetizers through dim sum to duck, fish and bean curd.
✉ 18 East Broadway ☎ 212/941 0911 🕐 Breakfast, lunch and dinner
🚇 Canal Street

GREAT NY NOODLE TOWN ($)
Noodles in innumerable forms and with an immense choice of meat, seafood and vegetables to accompany them.
✉ 28 Bowery ☎ 212/349 0923 🕐 Breakfast, lunch and dinner
🚇 Grand Street

HSF ($)
One of the better stops for lunchtime dim sum.
✉ 46 Bowery ☎ 212/374 1319 🕙 Breakfast, lunch and dinner
🚇 Canal Street

JOE'S SHANGHAI ($)
Range of Shanghai dishes but best known for its steamed buns, a selection of which make an inexpensive snack or a fuller meal, eaten from shared tables.
✉ 9 Pell Street ☎ 212/233 8888 🕙 Lunch, dinner 🚇 Canal Street

MANDARIN COURT ($)

A lively spot for lunchtime dim sum.

✉ 61 Mott Street ☎ 212/608 3838 🕐 Lunch, dinner 🚇 Canal Street

PHO BANG ($–$$)

Vietnamese food with variations of Pho, or beef noodles.

✉ 157 Mott Street ☎ Lunch and dinner 🕐 212/966 3797 🚇 Canal Street

VIET-NAM ($)

Hole-in-the-wall Vietnamese eatery with a great-value menu.

✉ 11 Doyers Street ☎ 212/693 0725 🕐 Lunch, dinner 🚇 Canal Street

EAST VILLAGE AND LOWER EAST SIDE

ACME BAR AND GRILL ($$)

Meat and fish dishes given a spicy Cajun treatment.

✉ 9 Great Jones Street ☎ 212/420 1934 🕐 Lunch, dinner 🚇 Bleecker Street

GREAT JONES CAFÉ ($$)

Red beans and rice, burgers, sandwiches plus other staples

served to the accompaniment of a pulsating jukebox.
✉ 54 Great Jones Street ☎ 212/674 9304 🕐 Dinner only
Ⓜ Bleecker Street

JULES ($$)
Modeled on a French bistro and serving simple but satisfying
French-influenced fare. Live jazz each evening.
✉ 65 St Mark's Place ☎ 212/477 5560 🕐 Lunch, dinner Ⓜ Astor
Place

ST DYMPHNA'S BAR AND RESTAURANT ($–$$)
Some of the best modern Irish cuisine at a tempting price.
✉ 118 St Marks Place ☎ 212/254 6636 🕐 Lunch, dinner Ⓜ Astor
Place

FINANCIAL DISTRICT, LITTLE ITALY, SOHO AND TRIBECA
BENNIE'S THAI CAFE ($)
Very affordable, very delicious Thai fare in a relaxed setting;
packed at lunchtimes with office workers but open until 9pm.
✉ 88 Fulton Street ☎ 212/587 8930 🕐 Lunch, dinner Ⓜ Fulton
Street

CHANTERELLE ($$$)

An elegant setting for an elegant meal, make a reservation well in advance for one this longest-established upscale eatery.

✉ 2 Harrison Street ☎ 212/966 6960 🕓 Lunch, dinner 🚇 Franklin Street

MEXICAN RADIO ($)

Great value Mexican food served with a selection of fiery sauces in a tiny eatery that makes a great hideaway when exploring Little Italy and SoHo.

✉ 19 Cleveland Place ☎ 212/343 0140 🕓 Lunch, dinner 🚇 Spring Street–Lafayette Street

SALAAM BOMBAY ($$)

A cut above most New York
Indian eateries.

✉ 379 Greenwich Street ☎ 212/226
9400 🕐 Lunch, dinner 🚇 Chambers
Street

ZOE ($$$)

A bright, attractive SoHo loft setting and an inspired menu

✉ 90 Prince Street ☎ 212/966 6722 🕐 Lunch, dinner 🚇 Spring
Street–Broadway

GREENWICH VILLAGE

AUGUST ($$$)

Rustic venue for European influenced dishes.

✉ 396 Bleecker Street ☎ 212/929 4774 🕐 Dinner only
🚇 Christopher Street

BIANCA ($–$$)

Simple but delicious northern Italian fare.

✉ 5 Bleecker Street ☎ 212/260 4666 🕐 Dinner only
🚇 Broadway–Lafayette

CAFÉ LOUP ($)
Cozy French bistro with candle-lit tables and delightful service.

✉ 105 W 13th Street ☎ 212/255 4746 🕔 Daily Ⓜ 14th Street

CAFFÈ REGGIO ($)
Dark and atmospheric, this coffee house has been popular since 1927.

✉ 119 MacDougal Street ☎ 212/475 9557 🕔 Daily Ⓜ W 4th Street

CORNER BISTRO ($)
Unpretentious locals' hangout; great burgers.

✉ 331 West Fourth Street ☎ 212/242 9502 🕔 Daily Ⓜ Christopher Street

COWGIRL HALL OF FAME ($$)
Plaid-shirted staff ferry Tex-Mex fare and margaritas to diners seated beneath photos of legendary cowgirls.

✉ 519 Hudson Street ☎ 212/633 1133 🕔 Lunch and dinner
Ⓜ Houston Street

FISH ($–$$)

Serves seafood in many forms with a varying but always fresh selection; the lunch specials can be exceptional value.

✉ 280 Bleecker Street ☎ 212/727 2879 🕐 Lunch and dinner

🚇 Sheridan Square–Christopher Street

GOTHAM BAR AND GRILL ($$$)

Make a reservation for dinner at this long-trendy shrine to excellent eating; the fixed-price lunch is great value.

✉ 12 E 12th Street ☎ 212/620 4020 🕐 Lunch and dinner

🚇 14th Street–Union Square

HOME ($–$$)

Innovative takes on traditional American fare.

✉ 20 Cornelia Street ☎ 212/243 9579 🕐 Lunch and dinner

🚇 W 4th Street–Washington Square

JAPONICA ($$)

Spartan setting for Japanese fare.

✉ 100 University Place ☎ 212/243 7752 🕐 Lunch and dinner

🚇 14th Street–Union Square

MA MA BUDDHA ($)
Well served Chinese dishes.
✉ 578 Hudson Street ☎ 212/929 7800 ⏲ Lunch and dinner 🚇 Christopher Street

MARY'S FISH CAMP ($$)
Pretend-Florida fish camp that makes a great pseudo-rustic setting for an impressive range of fresh and inventively-prepared seafood; the daily specials are particularly good value.
✉ 246 W 4th Street ☎ 212/486 2185 ⏲ Lunch and dinner; closed Sun 🚇 West 4th Street

MINETTA TAVERN ($$)
Long-serving Italian eatery serving dependable food.
✉ 113 MacDougal Street ☎ 212/475 3850
⏲ Lunch and dinner 🚇 W 4th Street

ONE IF BY LAND, TWO IF BY SEA ($$$)
Fine setting for a romantic dinner.
✉ 17 Barrow Street ☎ 212/228 9280 ⏲ Dinner
🚇 Christopher Street

PINK TEACUP ($$)

Deep southern breakfasts featuring grits, bacon and sausages; also soul food dishes.

✉ 42 Grove Street ☎ 212/807 6755
🕐 Breakfast, lunch and dinner
🚇 Christopher Street

RISOTTERIA ($–$$)

Risotto is served here in 40 different forms.
✉ 270 Bleecker Street ☎ 212/924 6664 🕐 Lunch
and dinner 🚇 Sheridan Square–Christopher Street

SILVER SPURS ($)

Busy coffee shop .
✉ 771 Broadway ☎ 212/473 5517 🕐 Breakfast, lunch and dinner
🚇 8th Street–NYU

WHITE HORSE TAVERN ($–$$)

The watering hole where Dylan Thomas drank his last.
✉ 567 Hudson Street ☎ 212/ 989 3956 🕐 Lunch and dinner
🚇 Christopher Street

Where to stay…
Downtown Manhattan

THE CARLTON ($$)
Comfortable and elegantly furnished hotel a few blocks from
the hustle and bustle of Midtown Manhattan.
✉ 22 E 29th Street ☎ 212/532 4100; 1-800/542 1502 🚇 28th Street

CARLTON ARMS ($)
Each wacky, threadbare room is designed by a different
(unknown) artist and what the Carlton Arms lacks
in creature comforts (which is quite a lot) it
just about makes up for through its sheer
eccentricity. Expect bizarre fellow guests
and exceptionally low prices.
✉ 25th Street at Third Avenue
☎ 212/684 8337 🚇 23rd Street

CHELSEA SAVOY ($$)
In the heart of the increasingly trendy
Chelsea neighborhood and making a

comfortable base for exploring the highly-regarded restaurants and art galleries virtually on the doorstep, as well as being well-placed for the rest of Manhattan.

✉ 204 W 23rd Street ☎ 212/929 9535 🚇 23rd Street

CHELSEA STAR ($)

Small themed rooms with shared bathrooms and some of the lowest prices to be found on the edge of the fashionable Chelsea neighborhood and in the shadow of the Empire State Building; even cheaper are the four-bed dormitories.

✉ 300 W 30th Street ☎ 212/244 7827 🚇 34th Street–Penn Station

GERSHWIN ($–$$)

The Campbell's soup can autographed by Andy Warhol that sits in the lobby is just the start for a highly individualistic property where every room has a Pop Art theme.

✉ 7 E 27th Street ☎ 212/545 8000 🚇 28th Street

HERALD SQUARE ($)

Occupying the 1893 *Life* magazine building, with mementos of the publication easy to spot, the rooms are all spartan but with clean, tiled bathrooms. The main attraction is the inexpensive rate charged here.

✉ 31st Street near Fifth Avenue ☎ 1-800/727 1888; 212/279 4017

HOLIDAY INN DOWNTOWN ($$)

A rare hotel in Chinatown that makes the most of its limited space with well-appointed if modest rooms; some of the best-value Chinese restaurants are right outside the door.

✉ 138 Lafayette Street ☎ 212/966 8898; 1-800/HOLIDAY
🚇 Lafayette Street

HOWARD JOHNSON–34TH STREET ($$)

Branch of the nationwide chain that offers good value in a promising location just across from Madison Square Garden, a stone's throw from the Empire State Building and within walking distance of both Times Square and up-and-comimg Chelsea.

✉ 215 W 34th Street ☎ 212/947 5050; 1-800 633 1911 🚇 34th Street–Penn Station

LARCHMONT ($–$$)

Shared bathrooms help make the Larchmont an affordable base in the heart of Greenwich Village and for discovering the

city without the hustle and bustle common to Midtown Manhattan.

✉ 27 W 11th Street ☎ 212/989 9333 🚇 Sixth Avenue

PIONEER ($)

Very affordable, no-frills rooms in a SoHo location, the Pioneer is ideal for those on a tight budget and already acquainted with the city.

✉ 341 Broome Street ☎ 212/ 226 1482 🚇 Bowery

SOHO GRAND ($$$)

One of the pioneering hotels to bring Midtown Manhattan comfort and service to the chic confines of SoHo in the 1990s, its bar and eatery still draw neighborhood celebrities.

✉ 310 W Broadway ☎ 212/965 3000, 1-800/965 3000
🚇 Canal Street

TRIBECA GRAND ($$$)

Set around an eight-story atrium and consuming an entire block, this hotel almost dwarfs the neighborhood in which it sits. Atmosphere may be lacking but amenities are not, with luxurious furnishings, audio-visual entertainment centers, and free high-speed internet access in each room.

✉ 2 Sixth Avenue ☎ 212/519 6600, 1-877/519 6600 🚇 Canal Street

WASHINGTON SQUARE ($$)

Some rooms are small, but excellent value in good location; breakfast included.

✉ 103 Waverly Place ☎ 212/777 9515; 1-800/222 0418
🚇 W 4th Street

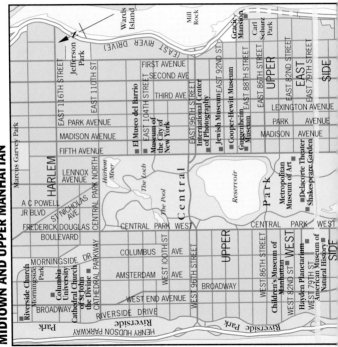

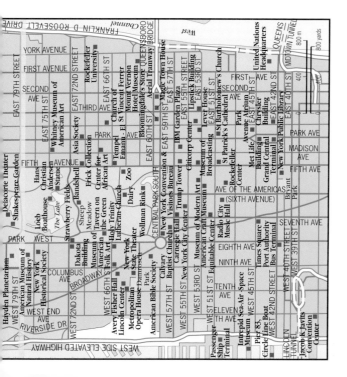

DISCOVER MIDTOWN AND UPPER MANHATTAN

Site of hotels and major attractions, Midtown Manhattan is where many visitors will find themselves staying and spending much of their time. While this effervescent area could consume your whole stay, a short bus or subway ride reveals more of Manhattan.

The heart of Manhattan is filled by the gloriously landscaped Central Park, an essential stop. East of the park, the Upper East Side accommodates Manhattan high society in elegant townhouses and luxury apartments. Framing the park's other side, the Upper West Side holds the American Museum of Natural History, reason enough to visit the area. To the north, Harlem is split between a predominantly African–American populated central area and East Harlem, main home of New York's sizeable Puerto Rican community.

AMERICAN MUSEUM OF NATURAL HISTORY

The American Museum of Natural History was founded in 1861 and, with roughly 36 million exhibits drawn from every corner of the globe, is now the world's largest museum.

The fossil and dinosaur halls are not only places to admire five-story-high dinosaur skeletons, but they also make the most of the state-of-the-art exhibits exploring the origins of life from the Jurassic period onward. Other representations of immense creatures include a fiberglass blue whale, the world's largest mammal, which sits above the other exhibits in the Hall of Ocean Life and Biology of Fishes.

Displays on humankind include halls for Native Americans and peoples of Africa, Asia and South and Central America.

Alongside the museum, a steel-and-glass cube provides a striking transparent exterior for the Rose Center for Earth and Space. Inside is the Hayden Planetarium and a series of walkways and galleries with displays on astronomical subjects.

✉ Central Park West and 79th Street ☎ 212/769 5100 🕐 Daily 10–5:45 🍴 Snack bar ($), cafeteria ($) and restaurant ($$) 🚇 79th Street or 81st Street ♿ Few 👊 Moderate

CARNEGIE HALL

With an intimacy that belies its international fame, Carnegie Hall was built with $2 million from the fortune of industrialist Andrew Carnegie and has been highly regarded ever since Tchaikovsky arrived from Russia to conduct on the opening night in 1891. Guided tours lead visitors around the horseshoe-shaped auditorium, its design modeled on an Italian opera house.

The adjoining museum provides a systematic account of the construction, and remembers many of the great artists who have appeared here.

✉ 154 W 57th Street ☎ 212/247 7800 ♿ Other than shows, interior

only on guided tours 🚇 57th Street ♿ Few ✋ Charge; museum free
❓ Guided tours Mon–Fri at 11:30, 2 and 3; museum Tue–Thu 11–4:30

CATHEDRAL CHURCH OF ST JOHN THE DIVINE

This is the largest Gothic-style cathedral in the world (it covers 11 acres) and yet, astonishingly, is still unfinished. The cornerstone was laid in 1892 but wars, the death of the architect, changes in design and regular shortages of finance have all played a part in causing the building work to be carried out in fits and starts. The most recent period of construction began in the 1980s after a 40-year hiatus. Temporary exhibitions fill the various nooks and crannies.

✉ 1047 Amsterdam Avenue
☎ 212/316 7540
🕐 Daily 7–7 Jul and Aug, 7–6 Sep–Jun
🚇 Cathedral Parkway
♿ Good ✋ Free

CLOISTERS

Medieval European monastic buildings might be the last thing anyone would expect to find in Manhattan, but this is just that. Assembled on a site overlooking the Hudson River, these bits and pieces of French and Spanish monasteries collected in the early 1900s now showcase the Metropolitan Museum of Art's medieval holdings. The contents are a feast of 12th- to 16th-century creativity, but the show-stealer is the setting, with its views and quiet atmosphere.

✉ Fort Tryon Park, Washington Heights ☎ 212/923 3700
🕐 Tue–Sun 9:30–4:45 Nov–Feb; 9:30–5:15 Mar–Oct 🚇 190th Street
♿ Good 👆 Moderate

COLUMBIA UNIVERSITY

The British king George II founded Columbia University in 1754, since when it has steadily moved northwards across Manhattan, arriving at its present site in 1897. The predominantly red-brick campus buildings, reflecting turn-of-the-century American collegiate architecture, are grouped around compact plazas.

Inside the Low Library (based on Rome's Pantheon), at the heart of the complex, are displays tracing the history of the university, one of the richest in the U.S. thanks in part to owning the Midtown Manhattan land on which Rockefeller Center now stands.

✉ 114th–120th streets between Amsterdam Avenue and Broadway
☎ 212/854 4900 🕐 Visit during daylight hours Ⓜ 116th Street
ℹ Visitor Center 213 Low Memorial Library ♿ Good ✋ Free

COOPER-HEWITT NATIONAL DESIGN MUSEUM

The museum, housed in the luxurious former mansion of steel mogul Andrew Carnegie, explores many diverse facets of art and design with outstanding temporary shows. Ceramics, wall coverings, textiles, drawings and prints form the bulk of the museum's stock of 250,000 pieces and the basis of most of the themed exhibitions. The collection began with oddments the three Hewitt sisters picked up on a visit to London in 1897.

✉ 2 E 91st Street ☎ 212/849 8400 🕐 Tue 10–5, Wed–Fri 10–9, Sat 10–6, Sun noon–6 🍴 Café ($) Ⓜ 86th or 96th Street ♿ Few
✋ Moderate

DAILY NEWS BUILDING

Better known to cinema-goers as the home of the Daily Planet and mild-mannered Clark Kent, alter ego of Superman, the Daily News Building is the base of the *Daily News* newspaper. Alongside an immense globe and a weather-measuring exhibit, the lobby displays some memorable front pages.

The architect of the building was Raymond Hood, a seminal figure in the creation of the New York skyscraper.

✉ 220 E 42nd Street 🕐 Lobby always open Ⓜ 42nd Street–Grand Central ♿ Good ✋ Free

DAKOTA BUILDING

Destined to be remembered by the world as the place where ex-Beatle John Lennon was fatally shot in 1980, the Dakota Building had nonetheless already earned a place in the annals of New York history by being one of the city's first purpose-built luxury apartment blocks. Raised in the 1880s, the Dakota steadily attracted the rich and famous to reside within its intensely Gothic façade, and remains a prestigious address.

✉ 1 W 72nd Street 🔵 Private residence; view from street only
🚇 72nd Street

EAST HARLEM

Since the 1920s, East Harlem has been the main base of the New York's Puerto Rican population and known locally as 'El Barrio'. Puerto Ricans' holding of U.S. citizenship, plus the start

of low-cost flights between the Caribbean island and New York in the 1950s, helped the city's Puerto Rican population expand to around 600,000.

The center of activity is between 110th and 116th streets on Park Avenue, where the stalls of La Marqueta (the Market) proffer sugar cane, yams and papaya, and other culinary delights of the island, while ghettoblasters send the sounds of salsa reverberating into the air. Although predominantly Puerto Rican, Cubans and Dominicans, and others from Latin America, also figure among the Spanish-speaking population.

✉ Loosely north of 105th Street & east of Fifth Avenue 🚇 110th Street or 116th Street

Puerto Rican Workshop, Inc.
Taller Boricua

EL MUSEO DEL BARRIO

Striving to link itself closely with the local East Harlem
community, El Museo del Barrio grew from a local school class
into a museum devoted to the cultures of Latin America,
particularly Puerto Rico. There is a small permanent collection
of pre-Columbian artifacts, but greater prominence is accorded
to many temporary exhibitions documenting facets of Latin
American history and culture. Paintings, folk art or sculpture
might be featured.

✉ 1230 Fifth Avenue ☎ 212/831 7272 🕐 Wed–Sun 11–5,
(Thu until 8) 🚇 103rd Street ♿ Few ✋ Donation

FRICK COLLECTION

Henry Clay Frick was perhaps the most detested of the self-made multi-millionaires who dominated U.S. life in the late 19th century, although his outstanding art collection draws many to his former mansion where the relative intimacy of the setting is as enjoyable as the paintings, sculptures and decorative items themselves. El Greco, Titian, Rembrandt and Turner are just a few of the painters represented by exceptional canvases, while two rococo delights – Fragonard's *Progress of Love* series and Boucher's *Arts and Science* series – each occupy a room of their own. Other highlights include Gainsborough's *The Mall in St James's Park* and Rembrandt's 1658 *Portrait of a Young Artist – Self-Portrait*.

✉ 1 E 70th Street ☎ 212/547 0700 🕐 Tue–Sat 10–6 (Fri until 9), Sun 1–6 🚇 68th Street–Hunter College ♿ Good ✋ Moderate

HARLEM

Many of the tens of thousands of
African–Americans who arrived in New York
in the late 1800s settled in brownstone
townhouses erected in Harlem by developers

anticipating an influx of affluent white residents from the Upper West Side. Instead, the neighborhood became the U.S.'s most culturally vibrant black urban area.

Partly dilapidated, partly gentrified, Harlem holds landmarks such as the Apollo Theater (253 125th Street) and several churches where gospel singing draws as many tourists as neighborhood faithful.

✉ North of Cathedral Parkway; west of Fifth Avenue
Ⓣ 125th Street

INTREPID SEA-AIR-SPACE MUSEUM

Seeing service in World War II and the Vietnam conflict, the aircraft carrier U.S.S. *Intrepid* is now spending its retirement years as a museum. Both the vessel itself, its workings and wartime exploits comprehensively detailed, and the many exhibits arranged around its decks, explore the changing face of warfare and document the technological innovations spawned by it. A former British Airways Concorde is among the civilian aviation exhibits. Temporary exhibitions cover related themes.

✉ Pier 86, W 46th Street ☎ 212/245 0072 ⏰ May–Sep, Mon–Fri 10–5; Sat and Sun 10–6; Oct–Apr, Tue–Sun 10–5 🍴 Café ($) 🚇 42nd Street ♿ Good 💲 Expensive

JEWISH MUSEUM

An imitation French Gothic château erected in 1908 for banker Felix M. Warburg provides an impressive home for the largest collection of Jewish ceremonial art and historical objects in the U.S. Among the enormous stock are household objects, coins and religious pieces dating back to the Roman era that help create a picture of Jewish life from early times to the modern day.

Many New Yorkers, both Jewish and Gentile, are drawn to the short-term exhibitions often presenting fresh perspectives on the Jewish experience.

✉ 1109 Fifth Avenue ☎ 212/423 3200 ⏰ Sun–Wed 11–5:45; Thu 11–8; Fri 11–3; closed public and Jewish holidays 🍴 Kosher café ($) 🚇 92nd Street ♿ Excellent 💲 Moderate

LINCOLN CENTER FOR THE PERFORMING ARTS

Part of what was the ghetto known as Hell's Kitchen and the setting for the musical *West Side Story* is now the multi-building complex of Lincoln Center for the Performing Arts. Since its 1960s completion, the center has provided homes for, among others, the New York Philharmonic, the Metropolitan Opera (the foyer of which is decorated by two immense Marc Chagall murals), the New York State Theater, and the celebrated Juilliard School for the Performing Arts, all grouped on or close to a central plaza.

✉ Broadway at 64th Street ☎ 212/875 5350

🍴 Various restaurants and cafés ($–$$$)

🚇 66th Street–Lincoln Center ♿ Very good

✋ Free to visit; charges for performances

❓ Daily tours; outdoor concerts in summer

MIDTOWN MANHATTAN

With its skyscrapers, department stores, high-class hotels, yellow cabs, hotdog vendors and bustling office workers, Midtown Manhattan is for many what New York is all about. Yet after the evening rush hour much of the area is remarkably empty, save for well-defined areas such as the theater district around Times Square (▶ 34–35).

The only deviation from Midtown's grid-style street layout is Broadway, which continues 140 miles to Albany.

✉ Loosely encompassing everything between 14th and 59th streets
🚇 Any serving Midtown

Walk

A WALK AROUND MIDTOWN MANHATTAN
Bisected by prestigious Fifth Avenue, in many ways this is the heart of New York City.

Start in Times Square.

Long a vibrant part of Midtown Manhattan, Times Square (► 34–35) and its immediate area has been transformed for the better. The completion of the New York Times building on the south side in 1904 gave the square its name.

Walk north and turn right into 44th Street.

The Millennium Broadway,

number 145 W, is among the many new luxury hotels to appear in the area; filling a whole block the lobby provides pedestrian access to 45th Street

Continue east along 44th Street.

This route brings you to the distinctive Metlife Building, adjacent to Grand Central Terminal (► 20–21).

Walk north along Park Avenue.

On the right is the Waldorf-Astoria Hotel, renowned

for pampering heads of state and other notables since the 1930s. The art deco features of the lobby merit a look.

St Bartholomew's Church, on the right, between 50th and 51st streets, was completed in 1919 by the celebrated New York architectural firm of McKim, Mead and White.

Walk two blocks west along 50th or 51st streets.

Its main entrance facing Fifth Avenue, St Patrick's Cathedral (► 134) was completed in 1878 in modified French Gothic style. Inside, the chapels and shrines glow in candlelight.

Walk west across Fifth Avenue, continue along 50th Street and turn right into Rockefeller Plaza.

With the skating rink (winter only) to the left and the GE Building to the right, you are in the heart of the Rockefeller Center (► 132).

Distance 2–3 miles **Time** 2–4 hours **Start point** Times Square
End point Rockefeller Center **Lunch** John's Pizzeria (► 148)

MUSEUM OF THE CITY OF NEW YORK

This museum tells of the city's evolution from Colonial settlement to international metropolis. Among the permanent exhibits are re-created interiors contrasting the spartan conditions of the city's early days with latter high-society elegance, glittering silverware which shows the skills of the craftsmen, and a gathering of dolls' houses.

✉ 1220 Fifth Avenue ☎ 212/534 1672 🕐 Wed–Sat 10–5, Sun 12–5 🍴 Café ($$) 🚇 103rd Street ♿ Few 🏛 Moderate

MUSEUM OF TELEVISION AND RADIO

The museum is a fabulous resource. Everything ever aired on U.S. television or radio is stored in the archives and made available from a computerized cataloguing system. Many items can be watched or listened to in private consoles, but most visitors will be content with the televisual selections screened each day and the choice of five audio channels carrying historic radio material.

✉ 25 W 52nd Street ☎ 212/621 6800 🕐 Tue–Sun noon–6, Thu noon–8 🍴 Café ($$) 🚇 Rockefeller Center ♿ Good 🏛 Moderate

NEW YORK PUBLIC LIBRARY

The city's pre-eminent reference library and an architectural masterpiece, New York Public Library is guarded by a celebrated pair of stone lions, symbolizing Truth and Beauty. Inside, the splendors of the design – such as the DeWitt Wallace Periodical Room and the wonderful mural lining the McGraw Rotunda on the third floor – are best discovered with the free guided tours. Various changing exhibitions in the side rooms, usually on themes of art and history, provide a further excuse to wander the magnificent corridors.

✉ Fifth Avenue at 42nd Street ☎ 212/930 0830 🕐 Tue and Wed 11–7:30, Thu–Sat 10–6 🚇 42nd Street

♿ Good ✋ Free ❓ Free guided tours daily 11 and 2, except Sun

NEW-YORK HISTORICAL SOCIETY

The hyphen in its name dates from the society's founding in 1804, a time when the city was spelled that way and when no other museum existed to receive the many bequests of wealthy New Yorkers. Consequently the society acquired a tremendous batch of art, from amateurish though historically important portraits of prominent city dwellers to seminal works by the Hudson River School painters and fine furniture from the Federal period. These items and much more fill several exhibition floors. Highlights include a substantial collection of Tiffany glasswork and the watercolors of John James Audubon's *Birds of America* series.

✉ 2 W 77th Street ☎ 212/873 3400
🕐 Tue–Sun 10–6 🚇 81st Street ♿ Good
✋ Moderate

RIVERSIDE CHURCH

Largely financed by John D. Rockefeller Jr., the French Gothic Riverside Church has loomed high alongside the Hudson River since 1930. Intended to serve its membership's recreational as well as religious needs, the church has at times held schoolrooms, a gym, a theater and even a bowling alley.

Originally Baptist but now interdenominational, the church's 392-foot-high tower houses the world's largest carillon, and has an observation level giving fine views across Manhattan's upper reaches.

✉ Riverside Drive between 120th and 122nd streets ☎ 212/870 6700 ⏰ Tue–Sun 9–5 🚇 116th Street ♿ Few 🎫 Free ❓ Observation deck; Sun carillon concerts; guided tours after Sun service

ROCKEFELLER CENTER

Bankrolled, as the name suggests, by industrialist John D. Rockefeller Jr. and spread across an 11-acre site, Rockefeller Center arose through the 1930s to become an admired complex of buildings that form an aesthetically satisfying whole, despite being designed by different architects.

Intended to provide a welcoming environment where people could work, shop, eat and be entertained, structures such as Radio City Music Hall and the RCA Building (now the GE Building) became city landmarks. The labyrinthine walkways have eye-catching art deco decoration while the Plaza, overlooked by a golden Prometheus, provides a setting for outdoor dining during the summer and becomes a skating rink during the winter.

✉ Bordered by Fifth and Seventh avenues, and 47th and 52nd streets ⏰ Always open 🍴 Various restaurants and cafés ($–$$$) 🚇 Rockefeller Center ♿ Good ✋ Free ❓ Expensive tours run by NBC ☎ 212/664 3700

ROOSEVELT ISLAND

Roosevelt Island is a long, thin strip of land between Manhattan and Queens and a curious piece of New York that few visitors ever become aware of. Reached by subway or a short cable-car ride (the so-called Roosevelt Island Tramway), the island once held 27 hospitals providing for the terminally sick and mentally ill.

The ruins of the old hospitals (enhanced by avant-garde sculpture) stand on the island's southern end, while much of the rest has been developed since the 1970s as a car-free housing development by architects Philip Johnson and John Burgee. Initially winning many plaudits, the scheme has faltered due to insufficient finance and political will, but the island makes for an intriguing detour, if only for the stunning views of Manhattan.

✉ East River, between Manhattan and Queens 🚇 Roosevelt Island; also cable car from terminal 60th Street and Second Avenue

ST PATRICK'S CATHEDRAL

Nowhere else in Midtown Manhattan is there a sense of peace and tranquillity matching that found inside St Patrick's Cathedral, at its best when its interior is illuminated by candlelight. The cathedral was completed in 1878 by celebrated architect James Renwick; the twin towers that rise to 330 feet were unveiled ten years later. This Roman Catholic cathedral, the largest in the U.S., retains its sense of majesty.

✉ Fifth Avenue at 50th Street ☎ 212/753 2261 🕐 Daily 7am–9pm
🚇 51st Street ✋ Free

SCHOMBURG CENTER FOR RESEARCH IN BLACK CULTURE

A collection that comprises over 5 million items spanning rare books, documents, audio and video tapes, film, art and other artifacts documenting the culture of all peoples of African descent. The centre also mounts strong exhibitions.

✉ 515 Malcolm X Boulevard ☎ 212/491 2200 🕐 Mon–Wed 12–5, Fri–Sat 10–5 🚇 135th Street ♿ Fair ✋ Free (moderate for exhibitions) ❓ Special events, drama

SEAGRAM BUILDING

Ground-breaking architecture is prevalent in Manhattan, but no single building is perhaps more influential than Mies Van Der Rohe's Seagram Building, completed in 1958 and widely regarded as the perfect expression of the International Style. Rising 37 storys in glass and bronze, the Seagram Building also gave New York its first plaza, a feature that subsequently became common with high-rise development, sometimes being enclosed to form atriums. Walk into the lobby to admire the Philip Johnson-designed interior and the celebrated Four Seasons restaurant.

✉ 375 Park Avenue ⏱ Lobby always open 🍴 Four Seasons restaurant ($$$) 🚇 Fifth Avenue ♿ Good ✋ Free

UNITED NATIONS HEADQUARTERS

The United Nations has been based in New York since 1947,
much of its administrative activity being carried out in the
unmistakable Le Corbusier-designed Secretariat Building rising
above the East River. Public admission is through the General
Assembly building, which holds internationally themed
exhibitions, and the ticket booth for guided tours, which
provide an informative hour-long sweep through the U.N.'s
interior. Outside, the 18-acre grounds hold parks, gardens and
abundant monuments.

✉ First Avenue at 46th Street 🕐 Guided tours daily; closed Sat and
Sun Jan and Feb ☎ 212/963 8687 🍴 Restaurant ($$$), café ($)
🚇 42nd Street–Grand Central ♿ Very good ✋ Moderate

UPPER EAST SIDE

Few New Yorkers of good breeding would feel right living
anywhere but the Upper East Side, the major residential
neighborhood of the rich and powerful since the 1890s when
the top names began erecting mock-European mansions
along Fifth Avenue, facing the recently finished Central Park.
Comfortable brownstone townhouses sprouted on adjoining

streets, now also dotted with smart apartment blocks.

In a parade of expense and pretence, Madison Avenue provides locals with antique shops, art galleries, boutiques, restaurants and dog-grooming specialists.

✉ East of Central Park between 59th and 105th streets 🚇 68th Street–Hunter College, 77th Street, 86th Street or 96th Street

UPPER WEST SIDE

The Dakota Building (▶ 110) set the tone for the Upper West Side and many more luxury apartment blocks through the late 1800s as residential development quickly filled the area between Central Park and the Hudson River. Decades of decline was halted during the 1980s with the arrival of yuppies seeking quality investments and liberal professionals fleeing the rising rents of Greenwich Village. Away from the quiet side streets, the commercial arteries hold a mix of furniture retailers, gourmet delis and fashionable ethnic eateries.

✉ West of Central Park, between Lincoln Center and 116th Street
🚇 72nd Street, 79th Street, 86th Street or 96th Street

WHITNEY MUSEUM OF AMERICAN ART

When the Metropolitan Museum of Art rejected her collection of American painting and sculpture in 1929, Gertrude Vanderbilt Whitney responded by creating her own museum.

Often controversial and devoting much of its space to relatively unknown work, the Whitney has an incredible collection of works by major names in U.S. art such as Rothko, Johns and Warhol. Three galleries are devoted to Calder, O'Keeffe and Hopper.

✉ 945 Madison Avenue ☎ 800/WHITNEY ⏰ Wed–Thu and Sat–Sun 11–6, Fri 1–9 🍴 Café ($) Ⓜ 77th Street ♿ Good 💵 Moderate ❓ Lectures, films

walk

A WALK ALONG FIFTH AVENUE & UPPER EAST SIDE

Long a byword for wealth and high social status, the Upper East Side is laced with 19th-century mansions, world-class museums and scores of prestigious shops.

Start in 65th Street.

The imposing 1929 Temple Emanu-El, on Fifth Avenue between 65th and 66th streets, has interior space for 2,500 people.

Walk east along 65th Street to the junction with Lexington Avenue.

The 1923 Church of St Vincent Ferrer has impressive stained-glass windows.

Walk north to 67th Street and turn right.

Across 67th Street is a corner of the Seventh Regiment Armory, an imposing red-brick structure, its drill hall now used for events. Ahead between Lexington and Third avenues is the crazed Moorish exterior of the 1890 Park East Synagogue.

Walk three blocks north along Lexington Avenue and turn west on to 70th Street.

Spacious St James Church (its entrance is on Madison Avenue) dates from 1884 but the handsome stained-glass windows and reredos were added in 1924.

Walk east along 70th or 71st streets to Fifth Avenue.

The Frick Collection (▶ 113) is housed in the former mansion of 19th-century industrialist Henry Clay Frick.

Walk north along Madison Avenue.

This section of Madison Avenue provides chic shopping opportunities for Upper East Side residents.

Walk east along 82nd Street to Fifth Avenue.

The Metropolitan Museum of Art (▶ 26–29) is entered by way of an awe-inspiring neoclassical façade.

Distance 2–3 miles **Time** 2–4 hours **Start point** 65th Street
End point Fifth Avenue **Lunch** Restaurant MoMA ($$)

Where to eat & drink...
Midtown & Uptown

MIDTOWN MANHATTAN

AQUAVIT ($$$)
In the main dining room root vegetable risotto and poached lamb loin are just two choices. Simple fare in the informal café.

✉ 13 W 54th Street ☎ 212/307 7311 🕐 Lunch and dinner; dinner only Sat and Sun 🚇 5th Avenue

BEN BENSON'S STEAK HOUSE ($$$)
As the name suggests, a carnivore's delight with everything from T-bone steaks and prime rib to veal and calves' liver.

✉ 123 W 52nd Street ☎ 212/581 8888 🕐 Lunch and dinner; dinner only Sat & Sun 🚇 7th Avenue

BROOKLYN DINER USA ($–$$)
Brash and enjoyable pseudo-traditional diner, with big breakfasts, bigger sandwiches, alongside burgers, assorted milkshakes, and the chance to round off the meal with a hot fudge sundae.

✉ 212 W 57th Street ☎ 212/581 8900
🕙 57th Street

CABANA CARIOCA ($$)
Major portions of Brazilian food
and a vibrant mood.
✉ 123 W 45th Street ☎ 212/581
8088 🕙 Lunch and dinner 🚇 Times
Square

CAFE EDISON ($–$$)
Off the lobby of the art deco Edison Hotel, this busy diner has
a full range of diner staples for breakfast, lunch and dinner,
with a few Jewish and Polish specialities also on the menu.
✉ 228 W 47th Street ☎ 212/840 5000 🕙 Breakfast, lunch, dinner
🚇 Times Square–42nd Street

CAFÉ UN DEUX TROIS ($$$)
The French bistro fare served here speedily is ideal for most
theater-goers.
✉ 123 W 44th Street ☎ 212/354 4148 🕙 Lunch and dinner
🚇 Times Square

CHENNAI GARDEN ($)

South Indian kosher vegetarian fare is served here; the extensive lunchtime buffet defies its absurdly low price, while ordering from the menu is barely less pricey; if in doubt sample the combination plates.

✉ 129 E 27th Street ☎ 212/689 1999
🕐 Lunch and dinner; closed Sun
🚇 28th Street

CHEVYS FRESH MEX ($$)

Part of a nationwide chain but a fun place for the family discovering Mexican food. There's a big list of fajitas, tortillas and much more.

✉ W 42nd Street ☎ 212/302 4010 🕐 Lunch and dinner 🚇 Times Square–42nd Street

DEAN AND DELUCA CAFE ($–$$)

A New York institution for their gourmet snacks, Dean and Deluca's quality nibbles

and hot drinks make a welcome find in this tourist area.
✉ 235 W 46th Street ☎ 212/869 6890 🕐 Breakfast, lunch and
dinner; closes 8pm Sun and Mon 🚇 42nd Street

DELEGATES' DINING ROOM ($$)

Armed with a reservation and proper attire, the public can rub
shoulders with United Nations officials and delegates (those
who eat here are unlikely to be famous faces) on any
weekday lunchtime. Top value is the buffet.
✉ United Nations, First Avenue at 46th Street ☎ 212/963 7626
🕐 Lunch only Mon–Fri. Reservations. ID required

ELLEN'S STARDUST DINER ($–$$)

Retro-diner packed with '1950s' memorablia and staff regularly
bursting into song; the menu offers classic diner fare such as
meatloaf, waffles, burgers and milkshakes but the theatrical
staff and setting are the draw.
✉ 1650 Broadway (at 51st Street) ☎ 212/956 5151 🕐 Breakfast,
lunch and dinner 🚇 50th Street–Broadway

FIREBIRD CAFE ($$)

Trade the New York street scene for a peek into pre-Revolutionary Russia with grilled sturgeon and chicken tabaka among the main courses served in a palace-like setting; the truly decadent might start with champagne and caviar.

✉ 363 W 46th Street ☎ 212/586 0244 🕔 Lunch and dinner; closed Mon 🚇 50th Street

FOUR SEASONS ($$$)

Inside the landmark Seagram Building and consistently rated as one of the best upscale dining experiences in New York.

✉ 99 E 52nd Street ☎ 212/754 9494 🕔 Lunch and dinner 🚇 Lexington–Third Avenue

JOHN'S PIZZERIA ($$)

John's thin crusts defined New York pizza from their original Greenwich Village base; whole pizzas or slices from this Midtown branch should match any in the city.

✉ 260 W 44th Street ☎ 212/391 7560 🕔 Lunch and dinner; closes 9pm Sun 🚇 42nd Street

MARS 2112 ($$)

Among the most imaginative of the city's many theme restaurants; diners mingle with extra-terrestrials while sampling 'inter-galactic fusion cuisine' that bears a surprising similarity to upscale American diner fare.

✉ Corner of 51st and Broadway ☎ 212/582 2112 ⏰ Lunch and dinner 🚇 50th Street–Broadway

THE SEA GRILL ($$$)

Cool blue decor creates a suitably ocean-like setting for the creations of one of the city's finest seafood chefs; choose from Chilean sea bass, crab cakes, mahi-mahi and lots more, inventively cooked and stylishly presented.

✉ Rockefeller Plaza, 19 W 49th Street ☎ 212/332 7610 ⏰ Lunch and dinner; closed Sun, dinner only Sat 🚇 49th Street

VICTOR'S CAFÉ 52 ($$)

Plantains, black beans, rice and other staples of Cuban cuisine, served with meat or fish in a lively setting.

✉ 236 W 52nd Street ☎ 212/586 7714 ⏰ Lunch and dinner 🚇 Seventh Avenue

ZEN PALATE ($)

Ultra-healthy vegetarian food in delicately arranged portions.

✉ 34 Union Square East ☎ 212/614 9291 🕐 Lunch and dinner
🚇 14th Street–Union Square

44 & X HELL'S KITCHEN ($$–$$$)

Traditional American fare given a fine-dining treatment:
meatloaf, waffles, steaks, and ribs all get a classy makeover;
service though can be brusque.

✉ 622 10th Avenue ☎ 212/977 1170 🕐 Dinner only 🚇 42nd Street

UPPER EAST SIDE

BROTHER JIMMY'S ($)

Sometimes rowdy spot for substantial sandwiches, soups and
barbecued ribs while watching sports TV.

✉ 1644 Third Avenue ☎ 212/426 2020 🕐 Lunch and dinner
🚇 96th Street

CIAO BELLA GELATO CAFE ($)

A hole-in-the-wall provider of sorbets, frozen yoghurts and ice
cream in myriad flavors, certain to cool and calm.

✉ 27 E 92nd Street ☎ 212/831 5555 🕐 All day 🚇 96th Street

DANIEL ($$$)

Immensely popular for high-quality French cuisine from one of the city's leading chefs.

✉ 60 E 65th Street ☎ 212/288 0033 🕓 Lunch and dinner
🚇 68th Street

MAYA ($$)

Delicious and flavorful upmarket Mexican main courses and inspired desserts; margaritas are smooth and potent.

✉ 1191 First Avenue ☎ 212/585 1818 🕓 Lunch and dinner 🚇 63rd Street

UPPER WEST SIDE

BARNEY GREENGRASS ($$)

Long-running Jewish deli with all the usual favorites, but best known for its delicious sturgeon and salmon.

✉ 541 Amsterdam Avenue
☎ 212/724 4707 🕓 Breakfast and lunch 🚇 86th Street

CAFÉ LUXEMBOURG ($$–$$$)

Lastingly popular French-style brassiere that draws knowledgeable diners to its eclectic, seasonally changing menu.

✉ 200 W 70th Street ☎ 212/873 7411 🕐 Lunch and dinner 🚇 72nd Street

EJ'S LUNCHEONETTE ($)

Simple canteen setting for no-nonsense breakfasts, sandwiches, burgers and milkshakes. All reasoanably priced.

✉ 447 Amsterdam Avenue ☎ 212/873 3444 🕐 Breakfast, lunch and dinner 🚇 79th Street

POPOVER CAFÉ ($–$$)

Pastry 'popovers' and a range of hearty soups, sandwiches and salads make this one of the neighborhood's most popular stops for a filling snack.

✉ 551 Amsterdam Avenue ☎ 212/595 8555 🕐 Breakfast, lunch and dinner 🚇 86th Street

Where to stay... Midtown and Upper Manhattan

DEAUVILLE ($$)

Appealingly priced well-furnished rooms and just right for a relaxing stay; occupies a 19th-century brownstone house just off the busiest Midtown thoroughfares.

✉ 103 E 29th Street ☎ 212/683 0990; 1-800/333 8843
🚇 28th Street

EDISON ($–$$)

Not only an affordable choice for the Times Square area but also a delight for art deco fans. Built in 1931 the 700-room hotel has a friendly ambience despite its size.

✉ 228 W 47th Street ☎ 212/840 5000 🚇 50th Street

EMPIRE ($$)

Trendsetting hotel offering small, well-furnished rooms all with CD, tape deck, color TV and VCR. The grand lobby displays a beautiful collection of model stage sets. Just a few steps from the Lincoln Center on Broadway.

✉ Broadway at 63rd Street ☎ 212/265 7400;
1-888/822 3555 🚇 66th Street

FOUR SEASONS ($$$)
Among the tallest and most opulent of the New York hotels,
each room cost an average of a million dollars to create and
comes equipped, among other things, with a voluminous
bathtub.
✉ 57th Street between Park and Madison avenues ☎ 212/758 5700;
1-800/487 3769 🚇 59th Street

HILTON TIMES SQUARE ($$–$$$)
In the pulsating heart of the Times Square district but with
quiet and sumptuous furnished rooms; at the inviting cocktail
bar, drinks are pricey but the wonderful views are free.
✉ 234 W 42nd Street ☎ 212/840 8222 🚇 Times Square–42nd St

HUDSON ($$)
Another Ian Schrager-owned, Philippe Starck-designed hotel
setting the pace for fashionable boutique hotels. Although
small, the rooms are torn from a design magazine's pages.
✉ 365 W 58th Street ☎ 212/554 6000 🚇 59th Street

MICHELANGELO ($$$)
The 18th- and 19th-century European art, marble and crystal help the Michelangelo rank among New York's most luxurious hotels.

✉ 51st Street at Seventh Avenue ☎ 212/765 0505; 1-800/237 0990
🚇 7th Avenue or Rockefeller Center

MORGANS ($$$)
Design-conscious lodgings from one of the creators of the legendary Studio 54, Morgans draws a fashionable crowd.

✉ 237 Madison Avenue ☎ 212/ 686 0300; 1-800/334 3408
🚇 33rd Street

THE MUSE ($$–$$$)
Discover what feng shui can do for a good night's sleep in this minimalist-designed hotel where a palm meter assesses new arrivals so they can be assigned a room of suitable color.

✉ 130 W 46th Street ☎ 877/692 6873
🚇 Times Square/42nd Street

THE NEW YORKER ($$)

This impressively restored 1930s art deco original has panoramic Manhattan views from many of its 800 rooms.

✉ 481 Eighth Avenue at 34th Street ☎ 212/971 0101; 1-866/800 3088

🚇 34th Street–Penn Station

PARK SAVOY ($)

Clean, comfortable rooms: the rates are remarkably low.

✉ 158 W 58th Street ☎ 212/245 5755 🚇 Columbus Circle

PLAZA ATHÉNÉE ($$$)

Luxurious rooms with European-style furnishings and with rose marble bathrooms; some suites have balconies.

✉ 37 E 64th Street ☎ 212/734 9100, 1-800/447 8800

🚇 Lexington Avenue

ROGER SMITH ($$$)

Tastefully furnished rooms, attentive service and sensible rates are the appeal of this hotel in a promising Midtown Manhattan location.

✉ 501 Lexington Avenue ☎ 212/755 1400; 1-800/445 0277

🚇 42nd Street–Grand Central

ROYALTON ($$$)

Impressive Phillipe Starck-designed interior.

✉ 44th Street between Fifth and Sixth avenues ☎ 212/869 4400; 1-800/635 9013 🚇 42nd Street

SALISBURY HOTEL ($$$)

Good-sized rooms with safes and refrigerators.

✉ 123 W 57th Street ☎ 212/246 1300; 1-888/NYC 5757 🚇 57th Street

WALDORF-ASTORIA ($$$)

A sightseeing stop for its opulent lobby and place in New York history for the accommodating of royals and heads of state.

✉ 301 Park Avenue ☎ 212/355 3000; 1-800/WALDORF 🚇 51st Street

WALES HOTEL ($$)

Long-serving hotel tucked away on the Upper East Side; includes a light breakfast and afternoon tea.

✉ 1295 Madison Avenue ☎ 212/876 6000; 1-866/925 3746 🚇 96th Street

WASHINGTON JEFFERSON (\$–\$\$)

Few frills and the cheapest rooms have shared bathrooms, but attractively-priced for Midtown Manhattan.

✉ 318–328 W 51st Street ☎ 212/246 7550; 1-888/567 7550

🚇 50th Street–Eighth Avenue

WELLINGTON (\$\$)

Except perhaps for the lobby, there is nothing fancy about the Wellington. Rooms are clean, simple and reasonably priced.

✉ Seventh Avenue at 55th Street ☎ 212/247 3900; 1-800/652 1212

🚇 Seventh Avenue or 55th Street

WOLCOTT (\$)

Modestly sized rooms at bargain rates.

✉ 4 W 31st Street ☎ 212/268 2900 🚇 28th Street, 33rd Street or 34th Street

WYNDHAM (\$\$)

Popular with Broadway performers. Good sized rooms at reasonable rates.

✉ 58th Street ☎ 212/753 3500 🚇 Seventh Avenue or 55th Street

Excursions

Immersed in the varied sights and sounds of Manhattan, it is easy to forget that the 22.7-square-mile island is only a fragment – albeit by far the most famous fragment – of New York City, which also comprises The Bronx, Brooklyn, Queens and Staten Island. That these four regions are rather dismissively known as the 'Outer Boroughs' is indicative of their low esteem in the eyes of many Manhattanites and the short-shrift they usually receive from New York visitors.

However, while they do provide dormitory accommodation for those who live and work in Manhattan, each of the Outer Boroughs has fought vigorously to maintain its own sense of identity, history and cultural worth and each, in its own way, has something special to offer the curious traveler. Certainly a visit to one or a number of them will provide a fuller picture of the real New York City.

THE OUTER BOROUGHS

From sites such as Yankee Stadium and Coney Island that resonate deep into the heart and soul of New York, to the high-quality displays of the Brooklyn Museum and the American Museum of the Moving Image, the Outer Boroughs contribute much more to city life than most visitors realise. With Staten Island, they also offer a welcome chance to find rural pleasures within the borders of the great metropolis.

There may be just four Outer Boroughs, but in terms of character and actual places to see each is entirely different from its neighbours. Lying north of Manhattan directly across the Harlem River, the Bronx fills an expansive area and requires several subway journeys to cross between its major points of interest. Queens, east of Manhattan, is even more far-flung: mile after mile of sprawling, tidy suburbia that conceals a great deal of ethnic diversity and numerous pockets of history. Like the Bronx, a trip to Queens requires careful planning and adroit use of the subway system.

Lying east and southeast of Manhattan, Brooklyn is much easier to reach and in many respects the easiest to explore of the Outer Boroughs. An impressive number of attractions lie close to the Brooklyn Bridge, linking the borough to Manhattan and simple to cross on foot; though sensible visitors might prefer to save energy with the short subway ride. Linked to Manhattan by a regular ferry service, Staten Island guarantees a peacefuLl few hours of pastoral exploration and is well covered by easy-to-understand bus routes.

THE BRONX

Spanning rundown areas such as the South Bronx, and comfortable residential areas, the Bronx tends to be neglected by visitors and New Yorkers alike. Nonetheless, with the Bronx Zoo and Yankee Stadium, the borough holds two of the city's major attractions as well as several minor ones, including the one-time home of author Edgar Allen Poe (East Kingsbridge Road) and the elegant 18th-century Van Cortlandt Mansion (Broadway between 240th and 242nd streets), built for a family prominent in politics and farming, now a showplace of English, Dutch and Colonial period furnishings.

BRONX ZOO

The largest city zoo in the U.S., the Bronx Zoo holds spacious replicated habitats inhabited by antelopes, rhinos, elephants, snow leopards, monkeys, gorillas and many more creatures from around the world. Nocturnal species can be observed in the World of Darkness area which turns day into night and

brings glimpses of foxes, aardvarks and bats going about their nightly pursuits. A 25-minute monorail ride provides an overview, and there is a children's zoo packed with furry creatures.

✉ Bronx River Parkway, Fordham Road ☎ 718/367 1010 🕐 Apr–Oct Mon–Fri 10–5, Sat and Sun 10–5:30; Nov–Mar daily 10–4:30
🚇 Pelham Parkway 🦽 Good ✋ Moderate

YANKEE STADIUM

Home of the New York Yankees baseball team since its 1923 completion, Yankee Stadium has seen tens of thousands of spectators thrilling to Babe Ruth and Joe di Maggio – and many less distinguished stars over the years – plus Pope Paul conducting mass in 1965. It now has a capacity of 57,000 (the stadium underwent a $100-million remodelling in the 1970s – its original cost was in the region of $2½ million), and its 11-acre site is scattered with memorials to Yankee greats.

✉ Junction of 161st Street and River Avenue
☎ 718/293 6000 ✪ Baseball season Apr–Oct
Ⓜ 161st Street–Yankee Stadium ♿ Good
✋ Variously priced match tickets

BROOKLYN
Only the East River divides Brooklyn from Manhattan but this so-called Outer Borough retains a distinct identity.

The pride of Brooklynites has been greatly dented by a series of economic reverses, made all the worse by the inexorable rise of Manhattan. The demise of the *Brooklyn Eagle* robbed the borough of its daily newspaper and the closure of the naval dockyards, which had employed 70,000 people in round-the-clock shifts, came in 1966. But perhaps the most symbolic sense of loss to many was with the move of the Brooklyn Dodgers baseball team to Los Angeles in 1955.

The popularity of the 1950s TV sitcom *The Honeymooners*, starring local actor Jackie Gleason, helped solidify Brooklyn's reputation as a working-class area of warm-hearted souls, though the image was a misleading one. Brooklyn has been an ethnically diverse community since its earliest days.

Brooklyn enjoys a reputation for its cultural institutions, such as the Brooklyn Museum and the Brooklyn Academy of Music, and with Coney Island holds an historic icon of New York life.

BROOKLYN MUSEUM OF ART

In keeping with the world-conquering attitude of 19th-century Brooklyn, the Brooklyn Museum of Art was conceived with no less an ambition than for it to be the biggest in the world. The exuberant beaux arts architecture that the revered New York firm of McKim, Mead and White created for the six-story museum between 1897 and the 1920s suggests its elevated goal, although the museum was only partially completed to its original plan due to the waning financial support that followed Brooklyn's absorption into New York City. The museum's 1980s renovation was the work of celebrated Japanese architect Arata Isozaki.

Now the seventh largest museum in the U.S. and in New York second only to Manhattan's Metropolitan Museum of Art, the Brooklyn Museum will easily consume several hours, if not a full day. The Egyptian collections alone are outstanding and include more than 500 items of stunningly decorated sarcophagi, sculpture and wall reliefs. Mosaics, ceramics and bronzes feature among the substantial horde of artifacts from ancient Greece and Rome, and 12 monumental reliefs from 9th-century BC Abyssinia form the core of the Middle East displays.

From more recent periods, a fine collection of paintings and period rooms highlight changing American tastes from Colonial times onward. Among the canvases are one of Gilbert Stuart's iconographic portraits of George Washington, painted in the 1790s. Impressive works from the Hudson River School artists culminate in Albert Bierdstadt's enormous evocation of nature in *Storm in the Rocky Mountains, Mount Rosalie*.

✉ Eastern Parkway at Prospect Park ☎ 718/638 5000 🕐 Wed–Fri 10–5, Sat and Sun 11–6, first Sat of month 11–11
🚇 Eastern Parkway–Brooklyn Museum ♿ Good ✋ Moderate

walk

A WALK AROUND BROOKLYN HEIGHTS

Tidy streets lined with brownstone houses and fabulous Manhattan views help make Brooklyn Heights one of the classiest neighborhoods in the Outer Boroughs.

Exit from Borough Hall subway station on to Joralemon Street.

At 209 Joralemon Street, Brooklyn Borough Hall has been the area's administrative base since 1802 but its current Greek Revival form dates from 1851. On the other side of Joralemon Street, the Brooklyn Municipal Building was completed in 1926.

Turn right into Court Street and left into Montague Street.

Lined by shops and restaurants,

Montague Street is the main commercial strip of Brooklyn Heights. On the corner with Clinton Street, the Church of St Anne and the Holy Trinity is a finely proportioned rendition of a Gothic church in local brownstone topped by a soaring spire. Finished in 1847, the church often stages musical and theatrical events.

Walk a block north to Pierrepont Street.

At 128 Pierrepont Street is the elegant home of

Brooklyn Historical Society (▶ 184).

Return to Montague Street and walk west.

Before the opening of the Brooklyn Bridge
(▶ 45), the western end of Montague Street
held the departure point for a ferry service to
Manhattan's Financial District, an excellent view of
which can be found along the Esplanade (also
known as the Promenade) running north from
Montague Street and lined with inviting benches.

*Follow the Esplanade north and turn right into
Orange Street.*

Immediately past the junction with Hicks Street
stands the Plymouth Church of the Pilgrims.

Distance 1 mile **Time** 1–4 hours **Start point**
Joralemon Street **End point** Orange Street **Lunch** Five
Front ($$) ✉ 5 Front Street ☎ 718/625 5559

BROOKLYN BOTANIC GARDEN

Occupying a one-time waste dump, the Brooklyn Botanic Garden fills 52 acres with 12,000 plant species. Passing magnolias and cherry trees, the footpaths weave through lushly landscaped surrounds linking the various sections. Perennial favorites are the Rose Garden, Herb Garden and the exquisite 1914 Japanese Garden complete with pond, stone lanterns and viewing pavilion.

Inside the three-part Steinhart Conservatory are plants from the world's deserts, rainforests and warm temperate regions, while fans of bonsai will find much to admire in the C. V. Starr Bonsai Museum.

✉ 900 Washington Avenue ☎ 718/622 7200 🕐 Apr–Sep Tue–Fri 8–6, Sat & Sun 10–6; Oct–Mar Tue–Fri 8–4:30 🚇 Eastern Parkway– Brooklyn Museum ♿ Few ✋ Moderate (free Tue Oct–Mar)

BROOKLYN HISTORICAL SOCIETY

With a $5 million restoration expected to continue for several years many exhibits, which span 9,000 artifacts, 100,000 graphic images, and more, all reflecting Brooklyn's history, will be shown in temporary exhibitions in locations around the city

The museum details chapters of Brooklyn's past with an engaging clutter of memorabilia and photography, all bolstered by clear and elucidating texts.

✉ 128 Pierrepont Street ☎ 718/222 4111 ⏱ Wed–Sun noon–5 (Fri until 8) Ⓜ Borough Hall or Court Street ♿ Few ✋ Moderate

NEW YORK TRANSIT MUSEUM

Housed in a former subway station, the New York Transit Museum holds the finely crafted art deco air vents and ceramic nameplates of the world's second-largest mass transit system. Walk-through subway cars from 1904 to 1964 demonstrate stylistic changes and technological innovations.

✉ 130 Livingston Street ☎ 718/694 1600 ⏱ Tue, Thu and Fri 10–4, Wed 10–6, Sat–Sun noon–5 Ⓜ Boerum Place–Schemerhorn Street ♿ Good ✋ Moderate

PROSPECT PARK

Manhattan's Central Park may be better known, but many Brooklynites regard it simply as a trial run for Prospect Park, laid out by the same design team of Frederick Law Olsted and Calvert Vaux through the 1860s. The 526-acre park encompasses lawns, meadows, streams and ponds, and provides the community with a bucolic space for jogging, strolling, picnicking, plus many special events throughout the year. In 1870, the park's main entrance gained the Soldiers' and Sailors' Memorial Arch, a triumphal marker to the fallen of the Civil War.

✉ 450 Flatbush Avenue ☎ 718/965 8999 (events) ⏱ Visit during daylight hours 🚇 Grand Army Plaza ♿ Few 🖐 Free

BRIGHTON BEACH

The decline of residential Brighton Beach more or less matched that of nearby Coney Island until the mid-1970s, when one of the unexpected results of the easing of immigration restrictions of Soviet Jewry was the arrival in the area of the first of what would become some 20,000 immigrants from the former Soviet Union. The initial slow influx became a flood through the 1980s and, following the collapse of the Soviet Union, still more arrived to join family members settled here. Cyrillic signs advertising caviar and vodka and scores of lively Russian restaurants are the main indications that this is the largest Russian community in the U.S.

🚇 Brighton Beach ♿ Good

CONEY ISLAND

Up until the 1940s, Coney Island not only promised New Yorkers a day by the sea for the price of a subway ride, but provided state-of-the-art fairground rides and peepshows and freakshows. Up to a million people a day flocked here to be seduced by the rollercoasters and rifle ranges, or simply to stroll the coastal Boardwalk munching a hotdog from the celebrated Nathan's Famous.

After decades of neglect, Coney Island has been revitalized and recognized as a living piece of Americana. Diverse exhibits are displayed at the Coney Island Museum, which also organizes local walking tours. Nearby, the towering Cyclone rollercoaster forms part of the thrills and spills offered at the Astroland Amusement Park. More sedate ways to pass the time include the greatly expanded New York Aquarium

✉ Surf Avenue between W 37th Street and Ocean Parkway
☎ 718/372 0275 🚇 Stillwell Avenue–Coney Island ♿ Good
✋ Museum moderate, Astroland expensive

QUEENS

With 2 million people spread across 119 square miles, Queens is in part all-American suburbia, but also holds an ethnic mix of long-established Italians and Greeks alongside more recently arrived Koreans, Indians, Chinese and Japanese. The neighborhood has a complex street numbering system that tends to confuse locals as often as visitors, though its places of particular interest are relatively easy to find.

The single area best representing Queens past and present is Flushing, which holds a large Asian population yet retains the Friends Meeting House (136–16 Main Street) and the nearby Bowne House that both date from the 17th century. In 1939, New York demonstrated its recovery from the Depression with a World's Fair in Flushing Meadows-Corona Park (immediately east of Flushing), its success prompting a second fair in 1964. Among the surviving items are Philip Johnson's New York State Pavilion Building and the 140-foot-high Unisphere, depicting the earth and her satellites.

Lining the East River, Astoria is one of the world's largest Greek communities and claims countless Greek bakeries, cafés and restaurants. Curiously, in the days before the industry shifted to Hollywood, the nascent U.S. film industry was based in New York, and in 1919 the company that evolved into Paramount Pictures opened a studio in Astoria. The American Museum of the Moving Image now stands on the studio's site (junction of 35th Avenue and 36th Street). The museum records the era with costumes, props, film-making equipment and vintage movie posters, and features many more general exhibits on film and television themes.

STATEN ISLAND

Totally unlike any other part of New York City, Staten Island is dominated by hills, trees and greenery. Its slow pace and pastoral appearance could be reasons enough to visit, but it also holds a sprinkling of enjoyable historical sites, an excellent collection of Tibetan religious art and sees regular open-air events throughout the summer.

The island is linked to Brooklyn by the imposing Verazzano-Narrows Bridge – which greatly increased the island's population following its completion in the 1960s – and to Manhattan by the Staten Island ferry. Though much romanticized, the ferry is actually no more than a large boat but the views of Manhattan on the return journey, the Statue of Liberty, and the island's commercial traffic, can be exceptional – and the journey is free.

ALICE AUSTEN HOUSE

Given a camera by her uncle in 1884, Alice Austen went on to take around 8,000 photographs that provide a remarkable documentary of turn-of-the-century American domestic life. Despite the quality of her photos, Austen remained unknown and only shortly before her death in 1952 did her photos find wide attention, following the publication of some of them in *Life* magazine. A short film describes Austen's life and some of her possessions and photos fill this attractive bayside home into which the Austen family moved in 1868.

✉ 2 Hylan Boulevard ☎ 718/816 4506 ⊙ Thu–Sun 12–5; closed Jan and Feb 🚌 S51 ♿ Few ✋ Moderate

CONFERENCE HOUSE

The stone-built Conference House, originally known as the Billopp House and built for a British naval captain, dates from 1680. It earned its new name as the venue of the only attempt to broker a peace between the Americans and the English after the Declaration of Independence. Held in September 1776, the negotiations proved futile but provided an excuse to turn the building, which served for a time as a rat-poison factory, into a museum with period furnishings and an intriguing display on the failed talks.

✉ 7455 Hylan Boulevard ☎ 718/984 0415 🕐 Fri–Sun 1–4; closed mid-Dec, Jan, Feb and Mar 🚌 S78 ♿ Few ✋ Moderate

GARIBALDI MEUCCI MUSEUM

Later to become one of the founders of independent, unified Italy, Giuseppe Garibaldi lived on Staten Island for two years in the 1850s having been forced to flee his homeland. Employed as a candle-maker, Garibaldi lived in this house that then belonged to Italian-American inventor Antonio Meucci. Letters, personal items and other knick-knacks document Garibaldi's period of occupancy.

A companion exhibit describes Meucci's life and achievements, not least his inventing of the telephone – an idea he unfortunately failed to patent.

✉ 420 Tompkins Avenue ☎ 718/442 1608 🕐 Tue–Sun 1–5 🚌 S78 ♿ Few ✋ Free

JACQUES MARCHAIS MUSEUM OF TIBETAN ART

A Wheel of Life, incense burners, ritual objects and other items from the world's Buddhist cultures (all accompanied by informative explanatory text) are among the collection of curiosities gathered in this stone cottage designed to resemble part of a Tibetan mountain temple. The extraordinary stash began with the discovery of 12 Tibetan figurines in the family attic by the 12-year-old girl of the house, Jacqueline Norman Klauber, who later adopted the professional name of Jacques Marchais and expanded the collection until her death in 1947. This fascinating museum enjoys a lovely hillside setting; the Dalai Lama is just one visitor who left impressed.

✉ 338 Lighthouse Avenue ☎ 718/987 3500 🕐 Wed–Sun 1–5
🚌 S74 ♿ Few ✋ Moderate

RICHMOND TOWN HISTORIC VILLAGE

The fruits of 50 years of gathering and restoring 17th- to 19th-century buildings on a 100-acre site, the Richmond Town Village provides a telling peek into bygone days. Period-attired local history enthusiasts lead visitors around the buildings,

often furnished with their original occupants' possessions, describing the trials and tribulations of Staten Island life in times past. During summer, the craft workshops are staffed by blacksmiths, shoemakers and carpenters demonstrating the old skills.

The oldest of the many noteworthy buildings is the 1695 Voorlezer's House, a church, school and home for the lay minister of the Dutch Reform Church. The far grander Greek Revival Third County Courthouse dates from 1837 and functions as a visitor center. Across Center Street, the Historical Museum provides an absorbing overview of the island's changing fortunes and the industries, from brewing to oyster harvesting, that have underpinned its often fragile economy.

✉ 441 Clarke Avenue ☎ 718/351 1611 🕐 Sep–Jun Wed–Sun 1–5; Jul–Aug Wed–Sat 10–5, Sun 1–5 🚌 S74 ♿ Few ✋ Moderate

SNUG HARBOR CULTURAL CENTER

While its tree-lined lanes would be enjoyable to stroll in any circumstances, the 83 acres of Snug Harbor Cultural Center are also dotted with preserved 19th-century buildings. Several of them serve a cultural function: the Newhouse Gallery displays works by living American artists in changing exhibitions; and the Veteran's Hall is a venue of concerts and recitals. In summer, the South Meadow stages outdoor concerts while the attractive Sculpture Park is filled with interesting works. The Botanic Garden and a small Children's Museum provide more reason to linger in an area originally known as Sailor's Snug Harbor, created to provide homes for 'decrepit and worn out sailors'.

✉ 1000 Richmond Terrace ☎ 718/448 2500
🕐 Dawn–dusk 🚌 S40 ♿ Good ✋ Free

SHOPPING

DEPARTMENT STORES & SHOPPING CENTERS

BARNEY'S

New York's largest new clothing outlet for years has international designer names, make-up, accessories, household goods and expensive restaurants.

✉ 660 Madison Avenue ☎ 212/826 8900 🚇 60th Street

BERGDORF GOODMAN

When money is no object, New Yorkers come here to buy their clothes; a full range of accessories is also to hand. Bergdorf Men is directly across Fifth Avenue.

✉ 745 Fifth Avenue ☎ 212/753 7300 🚇 59th Street

JEFFREY NEW YORK

Less pretentious than its midtown counterparts and without the tourist bustle, Jeffrey's offers a great range of designer clothing for men and women and gains plaudits aplenty for its quality footwear.

✉ 449 W 14th Street ☎ 212/206 1272 🚇 14th Street–8th Avenue

BRADLEES

This huge emporium is packed with just about everything at knock-down prices; don't expect high quality, though.

✉ Union Square ☎ 212/673 5814 🚇 14th Street

LORD AND TAYLOR

This lovely, somewhat old-fashioned store is particularly good for shirts, sweaters, trousers and skirts. The Christmas windows, featuring animated figures, are a delight.

✉ 424 Fifth Avenue ☎ 212/391 3344 🚇 Grand Central

MACY'S

With ten floors and 500,000 items for sale, Macy's claim to be the largest department store in the world is entirely believable.

✉ 151 W 34th Street ☎ 212/695 4400 🚇 34th Street

MANHATTAN MALL

Aptly named, the nearest thing in Manhattan to an all-American shopping mall with a large array of well-known, mid-range stores spanning fashion, household, gifts, electronics, food and more.

✉ Sixth Avenue and 33rd Street ☎ 212/465 0500 🚇 34th Street

SAK'S FIFTH AVENUE

Top-notch clothing, linens and cosmetics for those who value quality and traditional good taste over the vagaries of fashion. Known (and rightly so) for its good service.

✉ 611 Fifth Avenue ☎ 212/753 4000 🚇 Fifth Avenue

TAKASHIMAYA

Expect to pay high prices for beautiful things at this elegant Japanese emporium which comes complete with an atrium and a traditional tearoom where jaded spirits can be revived and aching feet rested.

✉ 693 Fifth Avenue ☎ 212/350 0100 🚇 54th or 55th Street

ART & ANTIQUES

A LA VIEILLE RUSSIE

Quality antiques many of them representing the handiwork of the finest craftsmen of Tsarist Russia.

✉ 781 Fifth Avenue ☎ 212/752 1727 🚇 59th Street

ANNEXE ANTIQUE GALLERIES
Each Saturday and Sunday finds vendors and would-be buyers converging on this open-air space where the stalls groan under the weight of artworks, rugs, furniture, jewelry and more.

✉ 107–111 W 25th Street ☎ 212/243 5343
🚇 23rd Street

ANTEQUARIA TRIBECA
Glorious hoard of European 20th-century period furniture, specializing in art deco, ornaments and lamps.

✉ 129 Duane Street ☎ 212/227 7500
🚇 Chambers Street or City Hall

THE END OF HISTORY
High class glassware, mainly from America, Italy, and Scandinavia, representing the craft's major names.

✉ 548 Hudson Street ☎ 212/647 7598
🚇 Christopher Street

GALLERY 532 TRIBECA
Original Arts and Crafts pieces; Gustav Stickley furnishings; paintings, pottery, lamps.

✉ 142 Duane Street

☎ 212/964 1282

🚇 Chambers Street or City Hall

JANET BORDEN
Highly regarded showcase for emergent and becoming-established photographers; several other galleries lie within the same landmark SoHo building.

✉ 560 Broadway ☎ 212/274 1679 🚇 Prince Street

LEO CASTELLI GALLERY
A gallery renowned for bringing the work of abstract expressionist and pop art notables to a wider audience, and still offering their works to well-heeled collectors.

✉ 18 E 77th Street ☎ 212/249 4470 🚇 Spring Street or Prince Street

MANHATTAN ART AND ANTIQUES CENTER

Over 100 stores are grouped here under one roof to provide hours of browsing delight for the committed art and antique seeker.

✉ 1050 Second Avenue ☎ 212/355 4400 🚇 59th Street

MARGO FEIDEN

Well-established gallery with many quality drawings, but best known for Al Hirschfeld's wonderful theatrical caricatures. Worth a look even if the prices are beyond your budget.

✉ 699 Madison Avenue ☎ 212/677 5330 🚇 Lexington Avenue–59th Street

PACE GALLERY

Prestigious gallery for the heavyweights of modern and contemporary art; particularly noted for rising names.

✉ 32 E 57th Street ☎ 212/421 3292 🚇 59th Street

THE SHOWPLACE

There are 135 art and antique dealers and craft outlets under a single roof.

✉ 40 W 25th Street ☎ 212/633 6063 🚇 23rd Street

CLOTHES & ACCESSORIES

BANANA REPUBLIC
Good middle-of-the-road duds for men and women at affordable prices.

✉ 114 Fifth Avenue ☎ 212/366 4630 🚇 Union Square

BETSEY JOHNSON
Bold and colorful female fashions that fall just short of daring. Also at several other city locations.

✉ 251 E 60th Street ☎ 212/319 7699 🚇 59th Street

BROOKS BROTHERS
From overcoats to suits and shirts, conservative men's clothing rarely comes of a better quality than found here.

✉ 346 Madison Avenue ☎ 212/ 682 8800 🚇 Grand Central

CANAL JEAN CO
Brave the pulsating music and garish lighting for an exceptional horde of cut-rate jeans, sportswear, T-shirts, accessories, and more.

✉ 718 Broadway ☎ 212/226 1130 🚇 Prince Street

CARTIER

Gold, silverware and porcelain that is the stuff of dreams;
prices reach the realms of the phantasmagorical.

✉ 653 Fifth Avenue ☎ 212/753 0111 🚇 47th–50th Street

CHELSEA GIRL

Stocks most things wearable from the 1920s to the 1970s,
from silk dresses and lingerie to cashmere sweaters and
businesswear, plus attention-grabbing accessories.

✉ 63 Thompson Street ☎ 212/643 1658 🚇 Houston Street

DAFFY'S

Bargains galore for those prepared to hunt through the racks
looking for designer-label look-alikes. Also good for casual stuff.

✉ 111 Fifth Avenue ☎ 212/529 4477 🚇 Union Square

DARLING

A one-time Broadway theater costume designer takes a cue
from vintage fashions and creates much to impress in this
small shop, which also offers selected items from other
designers.

✉ 1 Horatio Street ☎ 646/336 6966 🚇 14th Street

DAVID WEBB

This is the place to select that special diamond, emerald, sapphire, or pearl, fashioned into rings, brooches or cufflinks.

✉ 445 Park Avenue ☎ 212/421 3030

🚇 59th-Street–Lexington Avenue

ELLEN CHRISTINE MILLERY

Stock of quality vintage clothing that spans the decades; the gathering of women's hats alone make a visit worthwhile.

✉ 255 W 18th Street ☎ 212/242 2457 🚇 18th Street

FAMILY JEWELS VINTAGE CLOTHING

Everything from 1920s evening gowns to 1960s miniskirts.

✉ 130 W 23rd Street ☎ 212/633 6020 🚇 23rd Street

HERMÈS

Top-dollar silk scarves, handbags, belts, and a well-stocked equestrian section to prepare for those horse-riding weekends.

✉ 691 Madison Avenue ☎ 212/751 3181 🚇 59th Street

INA

Imposing designer garments, shoes, and accessories for the lady with a full social diary, at reduced prices.

✉ 21 Prince Street ☎ 212/333 9048 🚇 Prince Street

MICHAELS' – THE CONSIGNMENT SHOP FOR WOMEN

Many well-heeled Upper East Side ladies sift through the designer names sold here at lower-than-retail prices.

✉ 1041 Madison Avenue ☎ 212/737 7273 🚇 77th Street

MORGANE LE FAY
Women's separates and dresses, bordering on the theatrical.
✉ 67 Wooster Street ☎ 212/ 219 7672 🚇 Prince Street

OMG
Top-name jeans at compelling prices; casual wear, accessories.
✉ 546 Broadway ☎ 212/925 9513 🚇 Prince Street

POLO/RALPH LAUREN

Top-notch tweeds, cotton shirts and everything else for the man about Manhattan.

✉ 872 Madison Avenue ☎ 212/434 8009 🚇 68th Street–Hunter College

THE SHIRT STORE

Discerning shirt wearers can choose from a choice of eight collars and have their chosen design made to order.

✉ 51 E 44th Street ☎ 212/557 8040 🚇 42nd Street–Grand Central

TIFFANY & CO

Legendary store with three floors of highly desirable crystals, gold and silverware, clocks and jewelry, all at prices to suit the rich.

✉ 727 Fifth Avenue ☎ 212/755 8000 🚇 59th Street

WEISS AND MAHONEY

Engrossing collection of military uniforms, combat fatigues, field jackets, parkas and other items of army, navy and air force clothing and accessories.

✉ 142 Fifth Avenue ☎ 212/675 1915 🚇 14th Street–Union Square

LEISURE

CLASSICAL MUSIC & PERFORMING ARTS

BAM
The Brooklyn Academy of Music specializes in major new
works across the musical spectrum.

✉ 30 Lafayette Avenue ☎ 718/636 4100 🚇 Lafayette Avenue

EUGENE O'NEILL THEATER
Among the biggest and best of the Broadway theaters.

✉ 230 W 49th Street ☎ 212/239 6200 🚇 50th Street

JOAN WEILL CENTER
Architcually stunning building that is home to the renowned
Alvin Ailey Dance Company, as well as several smaller dance
groups, in what is the largest dance-specific building in the U.S.

✉ Corner 55th Street and Ninth Avenue ☎ 212/767-0590
🚇 59th Street–Columbus Circle

METROPOLITAN OPERA HOUSE
The opera's October opening night is a major New York
occasion on the social calendar and the season continues until

April. Ticket prices vary greatly, but the least costly offer a very distant perspective.

✉ Lincoln Center ☎ 212/362 6000 🚇 66th Street–Lincoln Center

NEW YORK CITY BALLET

The season for this renowned company runs from November to February and from April to June, with a special performance of *The Nutcracker* held annually each Christmas.

✉ New York State Theater, 20 Lincoln Center Plaza ☎ 212/870 5670 🚇 66th Street–Lincoln Center

NEW YORK CITY OPERA

Next door to the Met, offering newer works, operetta and even the odd musical.

✉ Lincoln Center ☎ 212/870 5570 🚇 66th Street

NEW YORK PHILHARMONIC

The main season is from mid-September to May, but the highly rated Philharmonic also undertake a series of free summer recitals in each of the city's five boroughs.

✉ Avery Fisher Hall, 10 Lincoln Center Plaza ☎ 212/875 5656 🚇 66th Street–Lincoln Center

PALACE THEATRE

Major Broadway theater and home to some of New York's most extravagant extravaganzas.

✉ 1564 Broadway ☎ 212/730 3200 Ⓜ 49th Street

PERFORMING GARAGE

Long-lasting Off-off Broadway space noted for its avant-garde drama and performance art.

✉ 33 Wooster Street ☎ 212/ 966 3651 Ⓜ Spring Street

PUBLIC THEATER

Six mixed-sized theaters under a single roof and home to the highly rated New York Shakespeare Festival for six weeks each summer.

✉ 425 Lafayette Street ☎ 212/239 6200 Ⓜ Astor Place

SULLIVAN STREET PLAYHOUSE

Since 1960, venue for The Fantasticks, the longest-running musical in the history of American theater.

✉ 181 Sullivan Street ☎ 212/674 3838 Ⓜ Christopher Street

LIVE MUSIC

BAGGOT INN

Enjoyable venue for lesser-known folk bands and occasional rock acts.

✉ 82 W 3rd Street ☎ 212/477 0622 🚇 W 4th Street

BB KING BLUES CLUB AND GRILL

Part of the new-look Times Square has been the opening of this upscale music venue that focuses on blues, but also features rock, jazz and other genres.

✉ 237 W 42nd Street ☎ 212/997 4144 🚇 42nd Street

BITTER END

Veteran of the 1960s folk scene, this small, cozy room still features up and coming folk acts interspersed with rock, jazz and comedy nights.

✉ 147 Bleecker Street ☎ 212/673 7030 🚇 W 4th Street

BLUE NOTE

Major jazz stars frequent this atmospheric club which can be very pricy to get in to.

✉ 131 W 3rd Street ☎ 212/475 8592 🚇 W 4th Street

CBGBS
Launchpad for 1970s New York punk bands, still showcasing rising stars.

✉ 315 Bowery ☎ 212/982 4052 🚇 Bleecker Street

CORNELIA STREET CAFE
The basement of this Greenwich Village restaurant makes a pleasantly intimate venue for jazz, poetry readings and other events.

✉ 29 Cornelia Street
☎ 212/989 9319 🚇 W 4th Street–Washington Square

FEZ
Intimate and well-designed venue for jazz combos and sometimes more.

✉ 380 Lafayette Street
☎ 212/533 7000 🚇 Bleecker Street

IRIDIUM
Medium-sized venue showcasing accomplished jazz names.
✉ 1650 Broadway ☎ 212/582 2121 🚇 49th Street

IRVING PLAZA
Premier location for catching the rising international names of
the indie rock and club scene.
✉ 17 Irving Plaza ☎ 212/777 6800 🚇 14th Street–Union Square

KNITTING FACTORY
The cutting-edge sounds of jazz and funk and rock's avant-
garde percolate through this musician-friendly venue.
✉ 74 Leonard Street ☎ 212/219 3006 🚇 Canal Street

MERCURY LOUNGE
Venue for the best local and rising national indie rock bands.
✉ 217 E Houston Street ☎ 212/260 4700 🚇 Second Avenue

TRIBECA ROCK CLUB
Cozy atmosphere and a diverse nightly diet that might feature
rock, blues, heavy metal, country, hip-hop, acoustic acts.
✉ 16 Warren Street ☎ 212/766 1070 🚇 City Hall–Chambers Street

VILLAGE VANGUARD

Long-serving atmospheric jazz venue with a deserved reputation for hearing the choice talents.

✉ 178 Seventh Avenue South ☎ 212/255 4037 🚇 14th Street

NIGHTCLUBS

AU BAR

Fairly bland disco music draws a predominantly designer-dressed crowd to this well-established up-market club decorated with polo sticks and croquet mallets.

✉ 58th Street ☎ 212/308 9455

BAKTUN

Diverse nights should hold something to please for the discerning fan of house, drum 'n bass, and other electronic-based beats presented with multimedia trimmings.

✉ 418 W 14th Street ☎ 212/206 1590 🕓 Closed Mon, Tue 🚇 14th Street/Eighth Avenue

BLUR

Not one to excite cutting-edge clubbers but when the sun goes down and until shortly before it comes up, Blur is a place for the unpretentious crowd to dance to chart and house music.

✉ 286 Spring Street
☎ 212/929 8560 🚇 Spring Street or Houston

COPACABANA

A new location for a legendary 1940s supper/cabaret club in which every top singer appeared, most fun for the steamy, smartly dressed Latin disco on Tuesday and Saturday nights.

✉ 226 E 54th Street ☎ 212/239 2672 🚇 59th Street–Columbus Circle

NELL'S

Comfortable, split-level dance club that draws a mixed crowd. Two main rooms spin anything from jungle to 1980s pop.

✉ 246 W 14th Street ☎ 212/675 1567 🚇 14th Street

ROXY

Cavernous Chelsea dance club that varies by night from gay to mainstream to Latin; becomes a roller-skating rink some midweek nights.

✉ 515 W 18th Street ☎ 212/645 5156 🚇 23rd Street–Eighth Avenue

SAPPHIRE

By club standards, a long-time survivor and pioneer of the nightclub invasion of the Lower East Side, with house, hip hop and rhythm and blues most nights.

✉ 249 Eldridge Street ☎ 212/777 5153 🚇 Second Avenue

SOB'S

The name stands for Sounds of Brazil and that, plus similarly infectious rhythms from Africa and the Caribbean, is what is delivered to a stylish crowd ready to dance the night away.

✉ 204 Varick Street ☎ 212/243 4940 🚇 Houston Street

SULLIVAN ROOM

Small basement club promising for techno and house music by some of the city's best DJs.

✉ 218 Sullivan Street ☎ 212/505 1703 🚇 4th Street

WEBSTER HALL

Lively and spacious venue with contrasting sounds in myriad rooms, and different themes each night.

✉ 125 E 11th Street ☎ 212/353 1600 🚇 14th Street–Union Square

BARS

THE BIG EASY

A New Orleans theme bar on the Upper East Side with loud music and a generally friendly clientele around the long, curving bar.

✉ 1768 Second Avenue ☎ 212/348 0879 🚇 86th Street

BLIND TIGER ALE HOUSE
The looks of a pre-Prohibition tavern and a strong selection of microbrewed beers.
✉ 518 Hudson Street ☎ 212/675 3848 Ⓜ Christopher Street

CHUMLEY'S
The unmarked door (street number only) is a reminder of Chumley's origins as a prohibition-era speakeasy; extensive bar range and walls lined with pictures of famous ex-regulars.
✉ 86 Bedford Street ☎ 212/675 4449 Ⓜ Sheridan Square–Christopher Street

D.B.A.
Popular hangout for East Village arty types with minimalist décor and a good variety of beers.
✉ 41 First Avenue ☎ 212/475 5097 Ⓜ Second Avenue

HEARTLAND
Big, brash and often rowdy, but Heartland has a tremendous stash of locally brewed beers.
✉ 35 Union Square West ☎ 212/645 3400 Ⓜ 14th Street–Union Square

HUDSON BAR
Expensive martinis and more are served at New York's coolest bar, amid the Philippe Starck designed furnishings of the trendy Hudson Hotel.

✉ 356 W 58th Street ☎ 212/554 6000 Ⓜ 59th Street

MCSORLEY'S OLD ALE HOUSE
Smoke-stained wood panels and photos of old New York all add to the atmosphere of one of the city's longest-serving bars.

✉ 15 E 7th Street ☎ 212/473 9148 Ⓜ Astor Place

PECULIER PUB
An enormous choice of beers and lagers from the U.S. and beyond are served here; Fridays and weekends draws a student crowd.

✉ 145 Bleecker Street ☎ 212/ 353 1327 Ⓜ Bleecker Street

SCRUFFY DUFFY'S
Prized for its oak floor, dart boards, pool table and friendly atmosphere, and also for its range of beers from near and far.

✉ 743 Eighth Avenue ☎ 212/245 9126 Ⓜ 50th Street

TOP OF THE TOWER

With the East River on one side and Midtown Manhattan on the other, few public places have a choice of New York views as does this elegant hotel bar.

✉ Beekman Hotel, 3 Mitchell Place ☎ 212/355 7300 Ⓜ 51st Street

WATERFRONT ALE HOUSE

Prides itself on its selection of malt whiskeys and bourbons, and also offers 50 micro-brewery ales from around the U.S. and beyond.

✉ 540 Second Avenue ☎ 212/696 4104 Ⓜ 33rd Street

WHITE HORSE TAVERN

Welsh writer Dylan Thomas is supposed to have drunk his last here in this attractive Village hostelry.

✉ 567 Hudson Street ☎ 212/ 243 9260 Ⓜ Christopher Street

CHILDREN'S ATTRACTIONS

AMERICAN MUSEUM OF NATURAL HISTORY (► 103)

BRONX ZOO (► 171)

BROOKLYN CHILDREN'S MUSEUM
Claimed to be the world's longest serving children's museum; entertaining and educational exhibits by the score.
✉ 145 Brooklyn Avenue, Brooklyn ☎ 718/735 4400 🚇 Kingston Avenue

CENTRAL PARK CAROUSEL
One of the most kid-pleasing attractions in New York: this vintage carousel revolves amid the greenery of Central Park.
✉ Central Park, just south of 65th Street Transverse 🚇 59th Street–Columbus Circle

CENTRAL PARK WILDLIFE CONSERVATION CENTER
Penguins, monkeys and bears are among the creatures in this 5½-acre chunk of Central Park; storytime each afternoon.
✉ 830 Fifth Avenue ☎ 212/861 6030 🚇 68th Street–Hunter College

CHILDREN'S MUSEUM OF THE ARTS
Young people aged from 18 months to 10 years can enjoy a creative play areas based around visual and performing arts.

✉ 182 Lafayette Street ☎ 212/941 9198 🚇 Spring Street

CHILDREN'S MUSEUM OF MANHATTAN
Explore the human body, nature, and much else.

✉ The Tisch Building, 212 W 83rd Street ☎ 212/721 1234 🚇 86th St

FAO SCHWARZ
Famous toyshop.

✉ 767 Fifth Avenue ☎ 212/644 9400 🚇 Fifth Avenue

MUSEUM OF THE CITY OF NEW YORK
Historic dolls' houses and vintage firefighting equipment.

✉ 1220 Fifth Avenue and 103rd Street ☎ 212/534 1672 🚇 103rd St

SONY WONDER TECHNOLOGY LAB
This outlet of the multinational corporation has regular multimedia programs for children.

✉ 550 Madison Avenue ☎ 212/833 8100 🚇 Fifth Avenue

WHAT`S ON WHEN

JANUARY/FEBRUARY

Chinese New Year: Parades in and around Chinatown; actual date accords with the lunar cycle.

Valentine's Day Marriage Marathon: Legions of couples tie the knot on the upper levels of the Empire State Building.

Empire State Building Run-up: Indoor joggers climb the landmark building by its stairs.

MARCH

Greek Independence Day Parade: Greek–Americans parade along Fifth Avenue between 59th and 79th streets to mark the regaining of their nation's independence in 1821.

St Patrick's Day Parade: Massive march of Irish and would-be Irish along Fifth Avenue, with countless related events.

MARCH/APRIL

Easter Promenade: A parade of outrageous Easter bonnets along Fifth Avenue.

Japanese Cherry Blossom Festival: Centerd on Central Park's Conservatory Garden and Brooklyn's Botanic Garden.

MAY

Martin Luther King Day: Memorial Parade Fifth Avenue between 44th and 86th streets.

Ninth Avenue International Food Festival: Celebration of ethnic cuisines between 37th and 57th streets.

Ukrainian Festival: In the East Village, Ukrainian food and cultural events marking the anniversary of the country's adoption of Christianity.

JUNE

Lesbian and Gay Pride Day: Enormous march along Fifth Avenue from Midtown Manhattan to Washington Square; many related events throughout Greenwich Village.

Puerto Rican Independence Day: Parade Along Fifth Avenue between 44th and 86th streets.

Shakespeare in the Park: Works of the bard staged for free in Central Park's Delacorte Theater, continues into August.

JULY

Independence Day: The biggest of the US's annual events celebrated with special activities throughout the city.

AUGUST
Harlem Week: Two weeks of special events marking Harlem's history and culture.

SEPTEMBER
Feast of St Gennaro: A 10-day festival based in Little Italy's Mulberry Street; stands dispense food and an image of the saint is showered with dollar bills.
Anniversary of September 11 World Trade Center attacks.

OCTOBER/NOVEMBER
New York Marathon: Begins in Staten Island and concludes in Central Park.
Macy's Thanksgiving Day Parade: Massive balloons paraded along Central Park West and Broadway.

DECEMBER
Lighting of a tree at Rockefeller Center marks the start of the Christmas season.

What you
need to know

Language Guide

The official language of the U.S. is English. New Yorkers, however, are a fascinating mix of cultures from all over the world and many different languages and dialects are spoken. Taxi drivers now have to pass a test before gaining their license and you should therefore be able to make yourself understood in either English or Spanish. Below are some words in common usage where they differ from the English spoken in the UK:

holiday	**vacation**		tap	**faucet**
fortnight	**two weeks**		luggage	**baggage**
ground floor	**first floor**		suitcase	**case or bag**
first floor	**second floor**		hotel porter	**bellhop**
second floor	**third floor**		chambermaid	**room maid**
flat	**apartment**		surname	**last name**
lift	**elevator**		cupboard	**closet**

cheque	**check**	banknote	**bill**
traveller's cheque	**traveler's check**	banknote (colloquial)	**greenback**
1 cent coin	**penny**	dollar (colloquial)	**buck**
5 cent coin	**nickel**	cashpoint	**ATM**
10 cent coin	**dime**	bill (restaurant)	**check**
25 cent coin	**quarter**		

grilled	**broiled**	biscuit	**cookie**
frankfurter	**frank**	scone	**biscuit**
prawns	**shrimp**	sorbet	**sherbet**
aubergine	**eggplant**	jelly	**jello**
courgette	**zucchini**	jam	**jelly**
maize	**corn**	confectionery	**candy**
chips (potato)	**fries**	spirit	**liquor**
crisps (potato)	**chips**	soft drink	**soda**

bonnet (of car)	**hood**	main road	**highway**
boot (of car)	**trunk**	dual carriageway	**divided highway**
bumper	**fender**	petrol	**gas, gasoline**
repair	**fix**	railway	**railroad, railway**
car park	**parking lot**	tram	**streetcar**
caravan	**trailer house**	underground	**subway**
cul-de-sac	**dead end**	single ticket	**one-way ticket**
lorry	**truck**	return ticket	**round-trip ticket**
motorway	**freeway**		

shop	**store**	nappy	**diaper**
chemist (shop)	**drugstore**	policeman	**cop**
cinema	**movie theater**	(colloquial)	
pavement	**sidewalk**	post	**mail**
subway	**underpass**	post code	**zip code**
gangway	**aisle**	ring up, telephone	**call**
toilet	**rest room**	long-distance call	**trunk call**
trousers	**pants**	autumn	**fall**

Practicalities

WHAT YOU NEED

● Required Some countries require a passport to remain valid for a minimum
○ Suggested period (usually at least six months) beyond the date of entry – contact
▲ Not required their consulate or embassy or your travel agent for details.

	UK	Germany	USA	Netherlands	Spain
Passport or National Identity Card where applicable	●	●	▲	●	●
Visa (regulations can change – please check before your journey)	▲	▲	▲	▲	▲
Onward or Return Ticket	●	●	▲	●	●
Health Inoculations	▲	▲	▲	▲	▲
Health Documentation (➤ 248, Health)	▲	▲	▲	▲	▲
Travel Insurance	●	●	▲	●	●
Driving Licence (national or international – national only for U.S.)	●	●	●	●	●
Car Insurance Certificate	○	○	●	○	○
Car Registration Document	●	●	●	●	●

TOURIST OFFICES

In the UK
NYCVB–London
33–34 Carnaby Street,
London W1F 7DW
☎ 020 7437 8300

In the USA
New York
Convention and Visitors
Bureau, 810 Seventh
Avenue, NY 10019
☎ 1-800 NYC VISIT

Times Square Visitor Center
1560 Broadway
(46th Street)
☎ 212/768 1560

CUSTOMS

YES
Duty-free allowances for non-U.S. residents 21 years of age or over:
spirits: 1 U.S. quart or
wine: 1 U.S. quart
cigarettes: 200
cigars: 100
or tobacco: 3 pounds or any proportionate combination.

Duty-free gifts: $100 provided the stay in the U.S. is at least 72 hours and that gift exemption has not been claimed in the previous six months.

You may include 100 cigars within this gift exemption, but not alcoholic beverages.

Articles must not be gift-wrapped as they must be available for inspection.

NO
Meat or meat products, dairy products, fruits, seeds, drugs, lottery tickets, obscene publications, chocolate liqueurs, fireworks, switchblade knives, firearms and Pre-Columbian artifacts.

WHEN TO GO

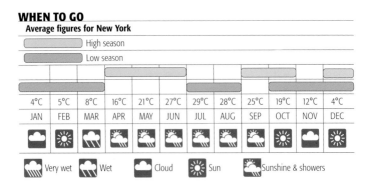

Average figures for New York

High season											
Low season											
4°C	5°C	8°C	16°C	21°C	27°C	29°C	28°C	25°C	19°C	12°C	4°C
JAN	FEB	MAR	APR	MAY	JUN	JUL	AUG	SEP	OCT	NOV	DEC

Very wet   Wet   Cloud   Sun   Sunshine & showers

ARRIVING

JFK Airport, Queens: Journey times: 'A' Train (via shuttle bus): 100 minutes approximately. Express bus to Grand Central Terminal: 60–75minutes. Taxi: 60 minutes (depending on traffic). Helicopter: 10 minutes.

JFK Int. Airport

16 miles to city centre

Journey times

N/A

60–75 minutes

60 minutes

Newark Int. Airport
New Jersey

15 miles to city centre

Journey times

N/A

40 minutes

40 minutes

MONEY

An unlimited amount of American dollars can be imported or exported, but amounts of over £10,000 must be reported to U.S. customs, as should similar amounts of gold. U.S. dollar travelers' checks are accepted with photo ID in most places (not taxis), as are credit cards, (Amex, Visa, MasterCard, Diners Card). Notes (bills) commonly come in 1, 5, 10, 20, 50 and 100-dollar denominations. One dollar is 100 cents. Coins are in 1-cent (penny), 5-cent (nickel), 10-cent (dime), 25-cent (quarter), 50-cent and (rarely) 1-dollar coins.

$5 $10 $50 $100

TIME

New York is on Eastern Standard Time, five hours behind Greenwich Mean Time (GMT-5). Daylight saving time (GMT-4) operates from early April (when clocks are advanced one hour) to late October.

INFORMATION

You will find other small information centers and kiosks at the airports, Grand Central and Penn stations and the Port Authority Bus Terminal.

Within the city are:
Times Square Visitor Center
1560 Broadway (46th Street)
☎ 212/768 1560
🕓 Daily 8–8
www.timessquarebid.org

Visitor Information Center
810 Seventh Avenue
(between 52nd and 53rd streets)
☎ 212/484 1212
🕓 Mon–Fri 8:30–6, Sat and

Sun 9–5
and kiosks at City Hall Park
and in Harlem at 163 W
125th Street
www.nycvisit.com

Useful Websites
Media:
The Daily News:
www.nydailynews.com
The New York Post:
www.nypost.com
The New York Times:
www.nytimes.com
The New York Observer:
www.observer.com
NY1 TV cable news channel:
www.ny1.com

City Government
www.nyc.gov

Metropolitan Transit
Authority
www.mta.nyc.ny.us

General information:
www.citysearch.newyork.com
www.newyorkmetro.com
www.zipbamboom.com

NATIONAL HOLIDAYS

JAN	FEB	MAR	APR	MAY	JUN	JUL	AUG	SEP	OCT	NOV	DEC
2	1	1(2)	(1)	1	0	1	0	1	1	2	1

1 Jan	New Year's Day	May	(last Mon) Memorial Day
Jan	(third Mon) Martin Luther King Day	4 Jul	Independence Day
		Sep	(first Mon) Labor Day
Feb	(third Mon) Presidents Day	Oct	(second Mon) Columbus Day
17 Mar	St Patrick's Day	11 Nov	Veterans' Day
Mar/Apr	Easter (half day Good Friday, Easter Monday whole day)	Nov	(fourth Thu) Thanksgiving
		25 Dec	Christmas Day

Boxing Day is not a national holiday in the U.S. Some shops open on national holidays.

OPENING HOURS

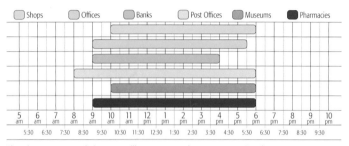

Shop hours vary greatly but open till 9pm on one day; some open Sunday noon–5. Some banks open till 3:30pm. Post offices open Saturday till 1pm.

There are over 2,500 places of worship in New York of every religious denomination – see Yellow Pages.

Opening times of museums vary, check with individual museums.

There is an all-night pharmacy at Duane Reade, 224 W 57th Street (☎ 212/541 9708).

PERSONAL SAFETY

Crime levels in New York have fallen sharply over recent years. Nonetheless, it is still wise to take sensible precautions:

Do not take the subway alone after midnight.

Do not walk quiet streets or Central Park alone after dark.

Carry only the cash you need, leave other cash and valuables in the hotel safe.

Report theft or mugging to the nearest police station; this will provide a refer-ence for your insurance company.

Police assistance:
☎ 911 from any phone

PUBLIC TRANSPORT

Public transit information (24hr) ☎ 718/330 1234. The $7 Fun Pass allows travel on buses (not express routes) and subways until 3am the next morning and is available from some MetroCard vendors (inc Times Square Visitor Center) but not at subway stations.

Trains The subway offers the fastest way to travel around New York. There are five main services which mainly run parallel along Manhattan's main avenues. Buy multi-trip MetroCards or tokens ($2 each) at the entrance to the stations and drop one in a turnstile to access the platform. PATH and MTA trains from Grand Central Terminal serve local stations beyond the city.

Buses The bus system is simpler but slower than the subway, but has the advantage of cross-town routes. Over 36 services operate, with stops every two or three blocks, indicated by bus stops with route numbers marked. Pay with MetroCards or tokens, obtainable at subway booths, or a flat fare of $2. Bus maps are available from the concourse of Grand Central Terminal.

Ferries The Staten Island Ferry runs a 24-hour service ☎ 718/815 2628, and Circle Line ferries run tours from Battery Park to Ellis Island and the Statue of Liberty, with magnificent views of the Manhattan skyline from the harbor.

DRIVING

Speed limit on freeways: **65mph**

Speed limit on all main roads: **65mph**

Speed limit on urban roads: **20–25mph**, depending on the area.

Compulsory for everyone in the front seats and for children in the back.

Drivers can be pulled over at random for a breathalyzer test (alcotest) by police. Zero tolerance is now the police code in New York.

Petrol (gasoline) is sold in American gallons. Five American gallons equal 18 litres. Most late-night and 24-hour gas (petrol) stations require you to pay the cashier before filling commences.

Driving is not recommended in Manhattan. Parking places are costly and difficult to find. If you break down with a rental car, call the rental company, or the breakdown number which should be prominently displayed on or near the dashboard.

CAR RENTAL

There are many car rental companies and prices are competitive; it pays to shop around. The main car rental companies have toll-free (800) telephone numbers, and airports and hotel lobbies will provide details. Expect to pay for unlimited mileage but not Collision Damage Waiver or Personal Accident Insurance. Special weekend deals are widely available, but you must be over 25 to rent a car. A full valid EU driving license is acceptable, or an International Driving Permit.

TELEPHONES

Making overseas calls from hotel phones can be expensive, doing so from public pay phones (widely found on the street and in hotel lobbies) is cheaper but will require a large amount of small change, except for the limited number of public phones that accept pre-paid phone or credit cards. Numerous cybercafes and other internet points offer email access at little cost.

International Dialling Codes
From the US to:

UK: 00 44	Germany: 00 49
Netherlands: 00 31	Ireland: 00 353
Australia: 00 61	

POST

Post Offices

The main branch of the U.S. Post Office is on Manhattan's West Side, at
421 Eighth Avenue/33rd Street. NY 10001. Open 24 hours.
Other post offices can be found in Yellow Pages.
Most are open 8–6 Mon–Fri, 8–1 Sat.
Mail boxes are on street corners. Hotel desks provide many mail services.

TIPS/GRATUITIES

Yes ✓   No ✗
It is useful to have plenty of small notes.

Restaurants (waiters/waitresses)	✓	15%
Hotels (chambermaids, doormen etc)	✓	$1
Bar Service	✓	15%
Taxis	✓	15%
Tour Guides	✓	discretion
Porters	✓	$1 per bag
Hairdressers	✓	15%

HEALTH

Insurance Medical insurance cover of at least $1,000,000 is strongly recommended. If involved in an accident in New York you will receive treatment by medical services and charged later.

Dental Services Your medical insurance cover should include dental treatment, which is readily available, but expensive. One emergency dental option (more are listed in Yellow Pages) is Travelers Medical Center ☎ 212/737 1212.

Sun Advice New York is very hot and humid in summer. It is wise to use a sunscreen and drink plenty of fluids.

Drugs Pharmacies dispensing prescription and over-the-counter treatments are on almost every block. If you need regular medication, take your own drugs and your prescription (for U.S. Customs). For out-of-hours emergencies several branches of Duane Reade are open 24 hours, including 224 W 57th Street (☎ 212/541 9708).

Safe Water Restaurants usually provide a glass of iced water. Drinking unboiled water from taps is safe. Mineral water is cheap and readily available.

ELECTRICITY

The power supply is: 110/120 volts AC (60 cycles). Sockets take two-prong, flat-pin plugs. Visitors should bring adaptors for their 2-round-pin and 3-pin plugs. European visitors will need either dual voltage facility or a transformer.

TAXIS

The New York Yellow Cabs are one of the sights of the city. When available for hire they display an illuminated sign on the roof and can then be hailed from anywhere on the street, though there are a few taxi ranks. They are legally bound to take you anywhere within the five New York Boroughs but you will be liable for bridge or tunnel tolls. Stretch limousines (with a driver) can also be booked at competitive rates if 8–10 people share.

CONCESSIONS

Students/Youths Students are entitled to discounts on many attractions. You will need to show proof of student status, with an International Student Identity Card, and evidence of your age.

Senior Citizens Senior citizens (seniors) will find discounts on many attractions. There are some variations to qualifying ages, ranging from 50 to 65. You will usually be asked to show your passport.

Some restaurants also have 'senior' discounts – it pays to ask.

Index

Index

ACKNOWLEDGEMENTS

The Automobile Association would like to thank the following photo libraries for their assistance in the preparation of this book.

Brand X Pictures 219; **Digitalvision** 212, 216; **Photodisc** 225, 239.

The remaining photographs are held in the Automobile Association's own Photo Library (AA World Travel Library) and were taken by the following photographers:

Douglas Corrance 10/1, 22, 28, 31, 38/9, 91, 131, 156/7, 166/7;
Richard Elliott 30, 32, 44, 54/5, 57, 66, 68, 69, 72, 80, 102/3, 105, 107, 113, 115, 116, 120/1, 126/7, 128/9, 133, 138, 142, 145, 168, 186/7, 188, 198/9, 209;
Paul Kenward 13, 25, 45, 104, 123, 140, 226; **Nicky Lancaster** 178, 179, 180;
Simon McBride 2tr, 2cr, 14/5, 18, 19, 21, 24, 26/7, 32/3, 61, 75, 83, 95, 146, 148, 151, 152, 162/3, 200, 230, 254/5; **David Pollack** 96; **Ellen Rooney** 36;
Clive Sawyer front cover, 1, 2tl, 2bl, 2br, 3b, 16, 23, 29, 35, 37, 46, 47, 48, 49, 50, 52, 53, 56, 59, 60 b/g, 60, 62, 64/5, 70, 71, 74, 77, 84, 86, 87, 89, 90, 92, 106, 108, 109, 110, 111, 114t, 114b, 118/9, 122, 124, 130, 132, 135, 136, 137, 155, 158/9, 160, 172/3, 174/5, 176, 177, 182, 183, 185, 190, 191, 192, 195, 197, 201, 202, 203, 205, 206, 208, 210, 220, 222, 232, 243, 246; **James Tims** 247.

Typesetting: **Information Engineers** Page layout: **Pentacor book design**
Editors: **Marilynne Lanng**, **Pam Stagg** Design support: **Katherine Mead**